AMERICA ON TRIAL!

by
Richard Koichi Tanaka

A Hearthstone Book

Carlton Press, Inc.   New

CONTENTS

Tables, Plates and Illustrations

DEDICATION

To Richard Inoru and Mae Yoshiko Tanaka

INTRODUCTION

The internment of 120,000 loyal Americans of Japanese ancestry during World War II stands as one of the great failures of American justice. *America on Trial* lays out the history that led up to the internment, and tells the story of those terrible days we spent in camp with clarity and passion.

I urge all Americans who care about the principle of equal justice under the law to read this book with care and attention. This work will endure as a testament to the dignity and loyalty of those who gave up their freedom to prove their loyalty.

Congressman Norman Y. Mineta, Member of Congress, 13th District, California.

PREFACE

If 120,000 American citizens were rounded up today and herded off to concentration camps, the public outcry would be deafening. No court in the land would permit it and no governmental body or newspaper would support it.

Yet in 1942, the United States government deprived more than 120,000 Japanese and Japanese-Americans of their constitutional guarantees of due process and without any fanfare forced them to leave their homes, farms and businesses. No individuals or organizations in any great number came to argue for the loss of their civil rights, since it was not a popular issue. These citizens and their families were subsequently sent to camps where most of them were interned for the duration of World War II, for approximately (30) months from 1942—1945.

To assume that this "just happened" even in those days of hysteria, and even after the devastation and "sneak attack" by Japan on Pearl Harbor, would seem unlikely, since reason and certain basic constitutional guarantees would not allow any mobilization of the mass movement of any particular ethnic segment of this nation only because of race. . . . What had happened subsequently to rationalize this blatant denial of due process by the U.S. government can surely be blamed to racism and economics, yet more importantly the lesson we learn from this infamous epic of American history, is that, if a selected segment of our society is allowed to create a hate campaign, however subtle at first, then able to continue the tactics of hate, eventually, there will be a time in history when this program of fear and racism can be orchestrated to create the logic and rational for any selfish movement. This is the sad legacy of that era.

In order to process the chronicle of events that lead up to this tragedy, one must review the beginnings of Japanese in America, follow their social behaviors, understand their language barriers and cultural traits that allowed the selfish and racist agriculturists and businessmen to exploit the Japanese and Japanese-Americans for exclusion from the West Coast. Untold devastation of the loss of properties and lives and the destruction of the family units were some of the initial outfall of this experience. Yet greater than that, the generations of Japanese-Americans will come to experience the trauma of "non-experience." Psychologists, as well as social scientists, only today are focusing in on this phenomenon of "non-experience," and its ultimate effects on the offspring of the first and second generation parents, their third generation siblings (Sansei) and also to some parents being part of the third generation, their fourth generation offspring, the Yonsei.

This, then is the theme of this book. What would be the real and permanent effects that would be ingrained in the Sansei/Yonsei offspring created by the non sharing ("non-experience") of the events and experiences of the parents in the "concentration camps" will be explored. This review will involve the intricate filial system and the various eastern cultural and social behavioral patterns, when permanently omitted, can prove to be a downfall of this proud race in the western world.

ACKNOWLEDGMENTS

I would like to give special thanks to my family, my wife, Barbara, my children, Craig, Todd, Sandra and Trent for their help, support and tolerance, as I researched and wrote and rewrote this book. Without their encouragement and help, these results could not be accomplished.

Special acknowledgements to the various persons who contributed to my book, and especially to the San Jose Commission on the Internment of local Japanese-Americans who helped me gather and permitted the use many of their in depth academic articles which were incorporated in this text. Gratitude to Bill Sullivan, Francis Higashi-Renteria, my wife, Barbara and daughter Sandra for the laborious task of editing the text.

I would like to thank Judge Wayne Kanemoto of the Kanemoto Collection for the generous use of his photographs that were incorporated in this book.

I would like to thank my daughter, Sandra Tanaka, for contributing her artwork which were incorporated in this book.

FOREWORD

This book was made possible due to the profound impact, awareness and rich experiences I gained from my grandfather and grandmother, Suekichi and Chino Koga and my father and mother, Richard Inoru, and Mae Yoshiko (Koga) Tanaka. Their directions and wisdom, their hard work, their spirit of "never giving up," and their countless sacrifices for our generation will forever symbolize the spirit of the Isseis and Niseis and their impact on the future generations of Japanese-Americans.

How often does an immigrant have to start over twice, to prove one's economic and moral commitment to America? Yet, immigrants from 1868 to 1941 were forced to lose all their worldly belongings, were displaced, incarcerated for nearly three years, losing their pride and destroying their moral fiber, because they happen to be Japanese.

Although true historical locations and names were used, my grandparents and parents as cited symbolize the countless Isseis and Niseis who have sacrificed their lives to make certain that the following generations would be given a better life than theirs. Therefore, all incidents depicted have not been fully documented as experienced by my grandparents and parents due to the fact that all information can no longer be verified due to the demise of both of my parents and my grandparents. Yet, it can be assured that the events and incidents are typical events that occurred prior to and after World War II.

After World War II (1945), the brave immigrants relocated to all parts of the United States and entered midstream America. Some never recovered from the trauma and economic losses due to their forced evacuation. Others did. Yet, to those "Quiet Americans", those 60,000 Japanese and Japanese-Americans who have passed on, and never will witness the day when America will apologize for the wrongs of misery, degradation, and economic losses placed on them due because of race, I dedicate this book.

AMERICA ON TRIAL!

Chapter 1
IMMIGRATION OF JAPANESE TO THE UNITED STATES

Immigration to Hawaii

No advertisement in the late 1860's had ever been placed in the Japanese newspapers to induce emigrants to the United States. The occasional articles and pictures in newspapers and magazines indicating success stories were the most effective means to encourage the emigrants to cross the Pacific to the new land.

The first contract workers arrived in Hawaii in 1868, consisting of 148 persons, against the wishes of the Japanese government. That was, also, the year that the industrial revolution began in Japan signaling the beginning of modern Japan. The nation economically shifted from agriculture to industry, and accompanying this phenomenon, a population explosion occurred. Industrialization resulted in new factories and jobs, yet could not absorb all of the displaced rural traditional farmers who made up the majority of Japan's population. This period in Japan's history is known as the Meiji Restoration Period.

Meanwhile, in California, the exclusionists with the support of the legislature successfully lobbied and helped pass the Chinese Exclusion Act of 1882, although the agriculturists later became cognizant of the fact that they needed part-time cheap labor excluded by this act to harvest their crops.

By 1886, Japan legalized emigration and the first generation

Japanese of approximately 200 persons per year during the years of 1886 through 1890 immigrated to America. The first immigrants were single men whose initial intention was not to permanently settle in this foreign country, but to make a "nest-stake" and return to Japan. Very few returned, and the majority of emigrants stayed, sought and married "picture brides" and began raising families in their newly adopted country.

The following *Table 1*, defines the Japanese arrivals and its population during the period from 1890 to 1940:

TABLE 1[1]
JAPANESE ARRIVALS AND POPULATION, 1890–1940

YEAR	ARRIVALS	RESIDENTS				PERCENT OF JAPANESE
	U.S. Mainland	West	California	Hawaii	On Mainland	
1890	691	2,039 (77%)	1,559 (57%)*	1,147	12,610	.003
1900	12,635	24,326 (96%)	23,376 (41%)	10,151	61,111	.03
1910	2,720	72,157 (94%)	68,150 (57%)	41,952	79,675	.08
1920	9,432	111,410	104,282	71,952	109,272	1.00
1930	837	138,310 (95%)	131,310 (70%)	97,456	139,631	1.00
1940	102	126,947 (95%)	120,927 (73%)	93,717	151,905	1.00

*The percentage of Japanese in West and California relative to the total mainland Japanese population.

The first generation Japanese, "Issei" worked very hard and subscribed culturally to good work ethics (one must work hard), not to offend anyone, not to be a burden to society, and above all, exercised acts and deeds that were honorable, thus insuring the preservation of not only the individual's good name, but also one's family and his relatives. With this philosophy and hard work, most Isseis were successful in the enterprises they initiated. Of the various ventures the Isseis were involved in, agriculture became their major avenue of livelihood.

In the late 1890's, Mitsuhei and Mura Tanaka left Kumamoto

prefecture, being only two of 691 Japanese leaving Japan during this decade. They bid farewell to their parents and set sail for Hawaii. The Tanakas' hearing of the great climate and a large population of Japanese already residing in Hawaii, suggested to them that Hawaii would not only offer an extension of the Japanese culture and its people, but further could afford great opportunities for the rural dislocated farmers of Japan. Due to these circumstances, Mitsuhei and Mura Tanaka on arriving in Hawaii, assimilated quickly with not only the Japanese population on the "Islands," but with the multi-ethnic population that started inhabiting the "Islands."

Mitsuhei Tanaka, soon after his arrival, started working in the sugar cane fields, but later was transferred to the refracting sugar cane factory. Long hours persisted, yet the benefits of the large paychecks eventually enabled the Tanakas' to make a down payment on a parcel of land near the beach at Waianae. Today, this portion of the Oahu's beachfront is the site of the famous "Banzai tube" surfboard competition.

Soon the industrious emigrant from Japan built his abode, went regularly to the Buddhist Temple on Sundays, and prepared to raise a family, which he reasoned would insure the continuity of the Tanaka namesake.

It was not until 1886, some eighteen years after the initial arrival of Japanese to Hawaii, that a formal agreement was signed between Hawaii and the government of Japan that allowed Japanese immigrants to immigrate to Hawaii in large numbers. By the 1900's, Japanese listed on the census in Hawaii numbered 61,111, which made up some 40 percent of the entire population of the Islands.

The Tanaka family consisted of Mitsuhei, father; Mura, mother; and eight sons and two daughters. The fourth son, Richard Inoru, was born on November 27, 1903. He was proud to be born in 1903, yet he often suggested that if he was born in 1906, all his offspring would remember his birth year since 1906 was the year of the great earthquake in San Francisco. Richard I., my father, had a normal childhood typical for most of Hawaii's Japanese-American lads during this era: He attended regular English school during the week, attended Japanese language school on Saturdays, then attended Sunday School at the local Buddhist Temple on Sunday mornings.

After school, the normal routine of a grade school student would be to walk the beach, swim in the ocean, climb a few palm trees and knock down some coconuts and generally got into normal mischief as expected of any young child only peripherally supervised by his elder brothers and sisters. To a child growing up in Hawaii, it must have reminded one that this must be "paradise." White shorts and bare feet were the normal attire, unless one was going to school, attending a public or a special event or attending a special appearance. What a life!

Immigration to California

The first Japanese immigration to California occurred on May 27, 1869, settling at Gold Hill, near Auburn in El Dorado County. The settlers were the iil-fated Wakamatsu Tea and Silk Farm Colony. Today, there exists a historical marker and monument commemorating this event. There are also some evidence that few Japanese were engaged in agriculture and horiculture in California prior to 1869. Yet, it was not until the late 1890's when a large migration occurred, and only then, did the Japanese start to have any impact on California's agricultural industry.

Whenever the Japanese returned from the United States for a visit or retirement to Japan, they all related their successes and experiences in the United States. They talked of coming to California penniless from Japan and due to hard work and the abundant untapped opportunities, everyone had the opportunity to amass great fortunes, which afforded the buying of hundred of acres of land for future use and the "good life."

Such commentaries and articles, many totally unfounded, appeared in the local newspapers and magazines of Japan. These accolades created strong impressions upon the young struggling farmer or country lad. Included in the wave of this enthusiasm and desire for success was a newly, young married couple, Sueikichi and Chino Koga. Hearing of these far-reaching success stories, and further fortified by seeing and hearing Mr. Kinya Uchizuma, the "potato king" of California, who appeared in public many times, the Kogas' as well many other future emigrants, decided to leave their homes. Sueikichi and Chino Koga rationalized that Mr. Uchizuma being well-known in their own Fukuoka prefecture, as well of all of Japan, all help validate that his testimony could be trusted.

In the early 1900's, Sueikichi and Chino Koga, two of the 12,635 persons leaving Japan during this decade, sailed out of Yokohama to California. Due to the heavy storm, it was reported that some travelers did not survive the trip. Most of the new arrivalees, including my grandfather and grandmother, assured that America was a land of riches, gathered all their worldly belongings, bid farewell to their respective parents and relatives and headed to the new world to make their fortune and a new life. It was reported that this trip took 21 days to sail the Pacific Ocean to San Francisco.

They landed in San Francisco and were processed through Angel Island. After processing, they proceeded to Santa Clara Valley which was in close proximity to the port of San Francisco. Santa Clara Valley, even at that time, was gaining a great reputation as an area of fertile soil and rich for agriculture. As noted earlier, most Japanese who left Japan during this era were rural Japanese farmers being displaced by the start of Japan's industrial revolution movement. Thus, Santa Clara Valley attracted many of the first Japanese emigrants to California.

Beginning of Farming

By 1890, a large group of Japanese started coming to this Valley in search for seasonal work and later stayed on to become independent farmers. Therefore, many of these laborers became tenant farmers, (share croppers) who made an agreement with the landholder to share in the income from the sale of the crops which was usually agreed as follows: 60 percent for the tenant farmer, and 40 percent for the landholder. Due to the many adverse factors such the banks not willing to approve the farmers' loan, even for seeds, or the need to borrow from individuals who charged usurial interest, or unpredictable weather, the Issei farmers in many instances became again, laborers struggling to repay their enormous debts.

The Issei farmers usually farmed and developed land adjacent to other Japanese orchards and farms in order to insure a greater sense of security from militant farmers and citizens and further by living in close proximity, helped bridge the gap of the language and cultural difficulties of this ethnic group.

Due to prejudice, distrust and language barrier, the Issei iso-

21

lated himself/herself from society, since he/she felt obligated culturally "not make waves," behave in a respectable manner," and further rationalized that this social behavior was appropriate, since he/she was a guest in this new country. The Issei reasoned: "What guest could create impositions on one's host," therefore vowed that if one must co-exist, one must avoid conflict, even though his/her pride and dignity may be taxed. This act of self-denial in Japanese is known as "gambaru." To translate "gambaru" means: Even though you may find an uncomfortable unjust situation occurring, it is a proud and honorable person who avoids conflict. Certainly this denial of action only applies to philosophical verbal charges, yet if life was threatened, "gambaru" becomes inappropriate.

The Issei had to struggle to survive either by working on his/her truck farms or his/her labor for others, yet never discouraged, found strength in his/her religion and culture. The unwanted visitor survived the harsh environment, secured homes, educated his/her offspring and created a sound foundation for all the Japanese-American generations to come. With the continual immigration after 1900's, the concentrations of farmers increased allowing the farmers collectively to hire and run the Japanese language schools which met on a weekly basis Monday through Friday at approximately 3:00 p.m. to 5:30 p.m. On Sundays, the community hall that housed the Japanese lauguage school during the week, was used for Buddhist services and Sunday School for the farmers' children.

It is noted as early as 1892, Dennis Kearney, one of the proponents for the Chinese exclusion, began charging that the cheap Japanese labor threatens the livelihood of all San Francisco's working force and in a major labor meeting on May 7, 1900, again raised the question for the need to extend the Chinese Exclusion Laws. He emphasized that the influx of cheap labor from the Orient would reduce job opportunities for all laborers. At the same assembly, then Mayor of San Francisco, James D. Phelan argued for the exclusion, as well as the San Francisco Chronicle, five years later, through their erroneous and misleading editorials supported and petitioned for legislation in Congress to stop Japanese immigration. Due to this law, Isseis were barred from American citizenship. Therefore, they were unable to participate in politics and found only a few champions for civil rights and

PLATE 1

Farming in San Jose, California, 1900 to 1906.
Courtesy Kanemoto Collection

justice who debated their plight, and were feebly protected only through Japan's diplomatic services.

By 1900, racial bigotry, exclusion and an orchestration of a systematic degradation of the Japanese in California started to accelerate. Logic leading up to these conclusions can be documented by a series of events, isolated at times, but which had the common theme of creating a campaign to remove the economic threat caused by the energetic ambitious Japanese immigrants to the United States.

The exclusionists started subtle innuendos, by stating that not only are California's Japanese winning the economic war, but also winning the baby war by producing more offspring than their white counterpart. The exclusionists failed to point out the Japanese females ranged from the late teens to thirty years of age (prime child bearing years) while the white females were twenty one or older.

By 1902, it was estimated that San Jose had over 200 Japanese in the permanent farming community and annually more than 3,000 Japanese seasonal workers passed through this area. The largest collective farming area owned and operated in San Jose at this time may have been in the area of North San Jose bounded by Coyote Creek the present Oakland Highway and lands on both sides of Trimble Road. The Japanese farmers who farmed in this area in future years will become known as "Trimble Road" area farmers.

From this date on, names not familar in San Jose prior to the 1900's, became strange familar ethnic names to the select public, especially those who desired to purchase the best, fresh, exceptional farm goods in Santa Clara Valley. Names like Koga, Tanaka, Nakamura, Inouye and Kotsubo were a few of the strange syllabled names the public must now try to pronounce with not too much success. At this time, Japanese farmers were producing pears, strawberries and a large quantities of other varied vegetables. Farming the "Trimble Road" farms at this time can be translated to be an occupation of hard work and long hours.

San Jose Nihonmachi

During this time in 1902, San Jose's Nihonmachi, (Japantown) was not exclusively the cultural and business area solely for the Japanese, since this area also included Chinese residences and

PLATE 2

Yamato Bath House, San Jose Nihonmachi, California, 1911.
Courtesy Kanemoto Collection

establishments; yet, due to the rapid growth of the Japanese population and an aggressive immigration program by Japanese, by 1909, seventy-nine various Japanese establishments flourished in San Jose's Nihonmachi. Establishments included Yamaguchi-ya (boarding house), Shiromoto Sakanaya (fish market), Kinokuniya Shoten (grocery store), Nihonjin Sentakiyo (Japanese laundry), Okita Brothers Store (general store) and others located in Nihonmachi.

Nihonmachi in San Jose satisfied the social and economic needs of the new Japanese immigrants. However, the immigrants soon realized that the most important element missing was a place to worship their Buddhist religion. In order to bridge this religious gap, the Japanese who left Japan a short while ago, started a movement to establish a permanent location to house their religion. Therefore, during the 1900's, the Buddhist Church in San Jose had it's beginnings, and on August 28, 1902, the San Jose Buddhist organization was recognized as a branch of the San Francisco Buddhist Church, with its ministers travelling to San Jose on a regular basis to conduct services and meetings.

Prior to 1907 and the construction of the first of three different structures to house the San Jose Buddhist Church, services were held at various homes on a routine basis. Farmers being very religious, faithfully organized and regularly scheduled these services and set aside Sundays of each week to worship and hold these services. (This act of holding a religious service with a small group of friends in one's home is known as "howai-kai.')

It was reported by 1910, farmers pooled their wealth and built a Sunday School Community Hall in the "Trimble Road" area for Sunday school and worship activities. A Buddhist minister, Reverend Takahashi, the first minister of the church, who arrived from Japan in 1906, had a busy schedule. Due to the increased activities of Reverend Takahashi, Reverend Gyoow Sasaki arrived in San Jose in 1907 to assist the Reverend.

After 1907, with the completion of the construction of the Buddhist Temple, it was reported that many farmers awoke earlier than normal on Sundays, completed their chores and labor in the fields by noon, and attended faithfully the scheduled afternoon services. This task was no easy matter, and it was further reported that irrigation and picking of produce were being done in the moonlight prior to the introduction of electric energy. This

PLATE 3

Original Buddhist Church, San Jose, California, 1902.
Courtesy Kanemoto Collection

insured the farmers the completion of their many chores, so that they could attend these scheduled church services.

Farming in California

In California by 1915, Japanese owned 16,449 acres, leased 80,232 acres and share cropped 59,000 acres. Although the Japanese owner-farmer decreased from 5,152 acres in 1920, to 3,956 acres in 1930, after the second generation "Nisei" came of age, this number increased to 5,135 acres in 1940, a net gain of 1,179 acres from 1930.

The Japanese farmers did not compete in farming activities of like crops with the white exclusionists farmers, yet animosities started to rise due to the great economic gains by the Japanese farmers involved in this labor intensive production of truck crops and berries. It is estimated by 1941, these crops returned approximately thirty to thirty five million dollars, and although representing a small portion of the total agricultural revenues, created in the minds of the white farmers a real threat to their future survival. Japanese farmers by 1941 grew 90 percent of California's beans, celery, peppers and strawberries, 50 to 89 percent of the artichokes, cauliflowers, cucumbers, spinach and tomatoes, and further started making definite inroads in the raising all truck crops grown in California. In addition to this, the Japanese became a leading producer of poultry and cut flowers, as evidenced that by 1941, 65 percent of the Los Angeles flower industry was controlled by Japanese horticulturalists.

As noted earlier, by 1915, Japanese controlled, owned and operated 155,772 acres of farming. Although this was small in quantity to the total farming acreage, the exclusionists were becoming aware of the future economic impact the Japanese may play on the total farming income. These phenomenal successes of Japanese Isseis and Niseis in California in farming created fear that the exclusionists' economic base in farming had eroded. This fueled their campaign to initiate their overt racial bigotry.

Further, in San Francisco, the Board of Education, in 1906, participated in the plight of prejudice against all Japanese, Chinese and Korean children, adding to international conflicts, by mandating these Asians attend oriental school in Chinatown. Such schools were permitted by state law, resulting in Japanese children as well as other Asian children being removed from the mainstream and placed in second class accommodations. These separationists' schools for Asians were permitted until 1946, when the state repealed that section of the Education Code. Therefore, the concerted efforts by various labor unions, farmers, school boards, heads of city, county, state governments as well as editors of newspapers all fortified and gave credence through acts, legislations and editorials from early 1900 through the advent of Pearl Harbor in 1941 that Japanese in California were not only a threat to our economy, but were taking jobs from whites and "sticking among themselves," not visible, or not participating in the greater society and therefore must be a menace to American society and the United States in general.

In 1913, under the protest of then newly elected President Woodrow Wilson, the 1913 Alien Law was enacted, permitting only aliens eligible for citizenship able to lease land under this act.

Following World War I, California exclusionists continued their verbal and written attacks on Japanese and Japanese-Americans. The founders of the Japanese Exclusion League, consisting of representatives of the American Legion, Native Sons of the Golden West, State Federation of Labor, and the State Grange, all campaigned to "Keep California White."

It is evident, from this time forth, Californians with the support of the Hearst press, started the repeated bombardment of the theme, the danger of the "yellow peril." Labor unions' concern for the elimination of cheap labor and the farmers perception of the threat of Japanese taking over the total agricultural enterprises, collectively, orchestrated the strategy for the removal of the Japanese population. This racist hate and fear campaign of the 1900's will initiate and be energetically carried on through the 1940's, giving the Army and the President of the United States a popular mandate in 1942 for the wholesale removal of citizens of our country due to ethnicity alone.

Chapter 2
JAPANESE SOCIAL STRUCTURE

Hierarchy

The hierarchy of social order formulated a comprehensive "natural law" for the Japanese society and became the extension of the family. The Japanese directed his/her everyday routines of behavior through these symbolization of languages and specific relationships. Therefore, the child understood at an early age, this social order. As a "natural hierarchy," it was quickly understood that some will govern and others would be governed, and that order could only exist if units acted as one. Thus, this important concept of "oneness" prevails throughout Japanese culture and society.

The following is a listing of Japanese hierarchy arranged relative to their order of importance, status, position and authority. The important and dominant person is on the left, and the right is subordinate:

kun-shin	emperor and subject
fu-shin	father and child
fu-fu	husband and wife
cho-ya	elder and junior
shin-tei	teacher and pupil

In a Japanese family, especially rural Japan the word "ie" meaning house, is a significant and profound concept. From this word, the Japanese derives the concept that house means family which includes not only one's immediate family but all of one's kinship. Therefore, it is understood that elders were to be respected, that the authority of "ie" was not questioned and individuals were committed to deeds that brought honor and respect to the family. "The filial duty of a son is a continuous obligation as long as the family is in existence. It is handed down from one generation to another. Fathers may not be fathers, but sons must always be sons, and they must be more pious than their fathers were to their forefathers."[2]

In 1930, sociologist Jitsuichi Masuoka, studying Japanese families in Hawaii, concluded that "the core . . . of Japanese family" is the body of sentiments which is clustered around the patriarch-heir relationship.

Masuoka states: "That the patriarch was the guardian of ancestry, land economics and family unity; his prominence was sanctioned by legal rights and unquestioned obedience. The eldest son was the inheritor of patriarchal status and therefore enjoyed a special respect and responsibility. The emphasis on male authority in terms of family inheritance was such that this relationship took precedence over even the husband-wife relationship—the bonds between mates were secondary to the bond between father and son."[3]

The Issei as well as the Nisei families' more pervasive Japanese value is that of filial piety. Filial piety from the Japanese point of view can be defined as the oath of empathy which links a person to the hierarchial order of the world. The ethical codes states: "Be loyal to your land, be filial to your parents." This unwritten loyalty and an unquestionable respect and honor for their parents have been ingrained on the sibling from birth. This moral and cultural value transcends to a greater issue, even beyond the love of family, its name and one as an individual. By these precepts, the Japanese individual must not cause shame to oneself since it affects not only one's family but also is extended to one's relatives and their offspring.

With regards to Japanese social behaviors, certain Buddhistic concepts such as "all that we are are the results of our actions," Karma, fortifies that siblings must do good deeds, must have good work ethics, must be contributors to society and community. The constant reinforcement of interrelationship of all things; judging of family by peers; importance of what others think of you; how well you are respected in the total community; all are important, and since "haji," (shame), can be transcended to the total family network, emphasis of proper individual conduct and morality are religiously practiced.

Suppression of individual's will or wants, the sense of one's efforts not creating a burden or embarrassment to others, explains in part, a Japanese cultural norm known as "enryo." Enryo involves a complex behavioral and cultural pattern which exercises restraint and respect for others, and assertiveness as required, which as times, becomes a contradiction.

Due to the emphasis in Japanese society on the hierarchy of the family; honor thy father, father as authority and his dominance to child; an unwritten law of exercising one's sensitivity for the feelings of others; all results in reactive opinions of the siblings who at times would had liked to express their thoughts, yet did not advance them. This behavioral pattern is contrary to the western mind! Thus, due to this behavioral pattern, the Japanese on many occasions is somewhat hesitant to express verbally his/her true inner feelings or opinions, since honor and preserving high esteem for his/her parents and nation do not allow one to embarrass these entities by erroneous comments.

In the winter of 1904, a son was born into the Koga family, the first son. What joy! Since he was a male son born in the United States, he was given an English name of George, as his first name and a middle name of Yoshio. Yoshio was the grandfather's father's name, and being oceans away from his parents, the naming of his son for his father, made him feel a little closer to his distant father in Japan.

The first son "chonan" (known in Japanese) was always ranked above the rest of children of the family, rightfully would receive special attention and education, and was delegated to serve as the head of the family and be responsibile with the duties and obligations concerning all family matters when the father passed on. Therefore, the heir apparent would naturally receive respect, honor and special treatment not only from his family but from the whole community.

He would be seated before other members of the family with the exception of his father. The younger children of the family were taught to respect their parents, elder brothers and sisters, relatives and even strangers. Any deviation of the above practice was not tolerated. The children were not allowed to answer "no," nor refute any of one's parents' commands. What they commanded, were to be obeyed. Younger children, too, were made to obey their elders. They had to call their elder brothers and sisters by certain titles, nisan (older brother) and nesan (older sister) and not by their given names. Thus, the eldest in the family are called by all his brothers and sisters, nisan or nesan instead of calling one's Japanese name, Yoshio, or by his English name, George. Being called Yoshio or George by any one of his younger brothers or sisters in the presence of the parents would, without doubt, result in a very fiery lecture or reprimands from them.

The eldest, could demand more things and had more privileges than the rest of the brothers or sisters. In this connection, the eldest as mentioned previously, had privileges not afforded to his younger brothers and sisters. At times, animosities were created by this unwritten law of the Japanese hierarchy. Question on this special treatment was usually quelched when one realized that the best should be given to the eldest son so that he would be able to maintain the good name of the family.

With the birth of George, grandmother had to leave the fields and stay home to nurse her first born son. It was a cold rainy winter, when George was born, and it was apparent that spring planting might be delayed due to this heavy unusual rain. With grandmother not being able to help, grandfather tended the fields alone, and thus needed to hire a temporary laborer. He journeyed into San Jose's Nihonmachi (Japantown) and inquired at the Nihonjinkai (Japanese organization) on the availability of Japanese laborers.

Soon, he was directed to a Kenichi Hamai, a former resident of Fukuoka prefecture, residing at the Yamaguchi-Ya, a local boarding house located on North Sixth Street. What luck! He went to the boarding house, asked the manager if Mr. Hamai was in. The manager stated he was at the Kinokuniya Shoten (grocery store) a block away on Jackson Street and was expected back within the next hour.

Grandfather, realizing that he could utilize his time more effectively, rather than by waiting, decided on visiting Yamato's Bath and Pool for a hot comfortable bath. Yamato's was a two story structure located on Sixth Street a few doors south of Yamaguchi-Ya. After explaining to the manager that he will be at Yamato's for a half an hour, he requested the manager inform Mr. Hamai, that he, grandfather will return shortly.

After grandfather completed his bathing, he returned directly to the boarding house, Yamaguchi-Ya and found Mr. Hamai under the exterior projecting second story balcony near the entrance to the boarding house. Grandfather approached Mr. Hamai, recognizing him by the earlier description given by the manager of his attire, and certain definite characteristics such as a beard and a wide brimmed straw hat, he was wearing. Grandfather could also be recognized easily, for my grandfather was a tall person in relationship to most Japanese. He was near 6 foot in height, husky and was known to dress like nobility; having his proper white shirt with cuffs, a bow tie and a black suit, (although this was his only suit he owned), one could not refute that his stature and physique created this air of nobility.

Grandfather, in speaking with Mr. Hamai, soon realized that they had mutual family friends in Fukuoka prefecture, and agreeing on the term of employment such as the monetary compensation, grandfather and Mr. Hamai got on his horse-drawn cart and headed for home.

In returning home, grandfather introduced Mr. Hamai to grandmother and she was pleased and grateful to find a willing hand especially from Fukuoka prefecture.

The following *Table 2* indicates the number of passports issued from each district in Japan during the five years from 1899 to 1903, the number of emigrants to foreign countries, including Korean and China is as follows:

TABLE 2[4]
GEOGRAPHICAL SOURCES OF IMMIGRANTS
1899-1903

Districts	No. of passports issued	Districts	No. of passports issued
Hiroshima	21,871	Fukushima	1,613
Kumamoto	12,149	Yehime	948
Yamaguchi	11,219	Aichi	767
Fukuoka	7,698	Fukui	683
Nigata	6,698	Shiga	646
Wakayama	3,750		
Nagasaki	3,548	Twenty-seven	
Hyogo	3,532	other districts	5,041
Okayama	2,176		
Miyagi	1,613		

Total immigrants 1899-1903: 84,576

Although the above statistics include emmigrants to foreign countries including China and Korea, more than 80 percent of the total number came to the United States.

The area of farm land cultivated by the Japanese in the State of California in 1908, noted on Table 3, and classified by their native districts are as follows:

TABLE 3[5]
FARM LAND CULTIVATED BY IMMIGRANTS FROM VARIOUS PREFECTURES

Cultivated by Immigrants from the district of:	Area of farm land in California—acres
Hiroshima	33,443
Wakayama	30,905
Fukuoka	14,833
Kumamoto	14,827
Yamaguchi	10,598
Aichi	10,268
Okayama	6,334
Other districts	33,592½
TOTAL	154,802½

35

Table 3, indicates that the immigrants from the district of Hiroshima cultivated the largest area of farm land in California, followed by the district of Wakayama. Each district controlled about one-fifth of all the farm land cultivated by the Japanese in California.

Although the immigrants from Fukuoka during 1899 to 1903 numbered only 7,698 compared to immigrants from Hiroshima of 21,871; farmers from Fukuoka controlled 14,833 acres, which represented the third largest acreage in California cultivated exclusively by Japanese immigrants. Due to the great influx of large number of Japanese from certain districts of Japan (*Table 2*) organizations started to be formed called "kai." The largest Japanese emigrant population came from the district of Hiroshima, followed by Kumamoto, Yamaguchi, then Fukuoka.

Grandfather, realizing the need to keep the ties with Fukuoka, soon gathered all the people he came in contact with, who were from this prefecture and helped organize and became one of the founding members of the Fukuoka Kenji-Kai. The outsider's perception of this forced "clannishness," by the early Japanese could be evidenced by the establishment of exclusive Japanese organizations such as the "kenjin-kai" groups composed of Isseis, which were organized from the same "ken" or prefecture; "sonji-kai", groups composed of immigrants from the same village; social welfare associations, such as the nihonjin-kai (Japanese organization) or later a more broad based business and professional organizations such as the Jackson-Taylor Professional and Merchants Association whose membership on the whole still would be composed mostly of people of Japanese ancestry.

Some of these organizations are still in existence today, since they still serve a function for the Isseis both culturally and psychologically, due to the ever present language barrier.

Isseis, through these organizations, eventually extended their family network to include all Japanese in California, and with these means satisfied economic and social concerns, therefore, now were able to place emphasis on their religion. This would ultimately satisfy the emotional needs of the immigrants. These social and cultural bonds were natural, since the immigrants collectively celebrated important religious celebrations, and having these common causes, formed associations which created a greater force to contend with in an ever growing unfriendly environment. Thus, by these various collective unifications by these immigrants, we find that the original social substructure of the "ken" (prefecture), being substituted to be "kuni" (country-Japan). Organizations encompassing all Japanese were soon being formed.

Kuni-Concept

The Issei now made a total effort to form the broadest "family" extension by the creation of the "kuni" concept. This satisfied the Issei's emotional self-confidence and gave independence to conduct one's economic ventures, without any external help from the greater community. This total ethnic, Japanese community concept further served and functioned to satisfy the racial, cultural and religious needs. The fulfillment of certain economic needs were harder to achieve.

Yet, to offset the concerns of the uncertain local economic and financial practices of many banking and financial institutions who summarily disapproved loans of Isseis, the Isseis looked for other sources to meet their financial needs.

Tanomoshi

One example for such a financial source was the "tanomoshi", a mutual financial group. Usual size of the group was approximately twenty members. Members of the group were heads of families and it was customary for the members to meet at least once a month at a selected family residence for the purpose of loaning from the pool of money derived from the regular fixed deposits by each member. Traditionally when the family received the loan, a party was held by at the recipient's home to thank the members for the loan. Although the tradition of becoming the recepient of the "loan" was through lottery, if an emergency arose for a certain member (medical, bank loan becoming due, or other serious situations), the recepient for the following month usually through courtesy, gave his/her turn for the "loan" to the more needy. Those members who did not have a need to borrow this money, or banked their portion of the "tanomoshi" funds, found that this became the very funds for their future visit to Japan.

Dr. Ogata points out that the "tanomoshi" worked on the basis of a monthly investment of members into a communal pot which was given to the highest bidder:

"Members agreed to put up a specified amount of money, say $5.00 to $10.00 per month. The promoter, or the person in charge of keeping accounts, took the first "pot." Beginning with the second month, the pot went to the highest bidder, (yet some "tanomoshi" clubs used a lottery system to select the following recipient to this "pot"). If the bid system was used, the bid was divided among the remaining members in lieu of interest. Once a person took the pot, he was no longer eligibile for dividends, therefore, the longer he refrained, the larger was his return."[6]

Due to these self-help organizations which satisfied many of the financial and social needs of the ethnic community, this practice also tended to create further isolation of the Isseis from the American scene.

Giri

One of the most important social obligation was the act of "giri." "Giri," simply means that there are certain reciprocal obligations between friends and acquaintances. This is an important factor in rural communities where reciprocal exchanging of goods and services were essential. It is important to point out that the act of "giri," although a free giving process by the givers, is a highly formalized practice. The value of gifts, labor or even emotions were carefully and exactly calculated and had to be returned or reciprocated at a given set time. Ogata, in "Kodomo no tame ni," gives an example of the precision of "giri" and would sometimes be measured to the dollar.

"As a marriage gift, received a twenty-five dollar Mix-Master from a family which has six daughters. It has the $25 price tag on it, but I suppose this was an oversight. In any case, every time anything very important happens in that family, I supposed to give in return something of as much or greater value. Soon the first of these girls will be graduating from college, and I will have to remember them at that time. Then they will be getting married, and I am supposed to remember that. If the daughters have babies, I must remember that. If the father dies, I have to remember that, or if any of them are sick, I am supposed to go to the hospital with some bottles of fruit juice. That is how complicated the exchange of gifts can become."[7]

Between very close friends or immediate family or relatives, the accounting is less exact, and generalized, yet an accurate accounting between friends was ethically expected.

Kosai
Another form of social obligation was the act of "kosai." This act established close human relationships and bond with neighbors, friends and relatives by bringing gifts on all occasions, whether it was a casual visit to one's home or a more formal wedding present.

Being an immigrant to this new land, the Issei was forced to share his common ethnic background with others of his race and generally was required to exercise economic dependencies with the help of other Isseis. Having a distinct language barrier, suspect in a new adopted country and the growing racial tensions, the Issei through necessity channeled his/her entire social structure to his/her own social commonalities and sought group cooperation for his/her socio-economic needs. Therefore, the prideful Japanese who ethically desired to be self-sufficient in the new country, "taking care of one's self," were now being accused of being "clannish" since more and more Japanese were only seen in various exclusive Japanese establishments or organizations.

Spring was late in arriving in San Jose as predicted by grandfather last winter, when George Yoshio was born; thus the preparation of the fields for spring planting would be late. Winter crops of broccoli, cabbage and cauliflowers had been harvested, yet following these crops the fields sat vacant. Rain, wet weather and muddy conditions did not allow for plowing, grading and leveling of the land; therefore, furrows could not be prepared for the irrigation of crops. Farmers knew civil engineering principles during this era, since they were able to grade their fields level, so that water flowed from one end of the field to another, without flooding or backflowing.

When the fields were seeded in late April, two months later than normal for spring crops, weather began getting warmer. Grandfather prepared a special cover over the horse drawn wagon hauler, (used to carry vegetables to the barn for washing before being sent to the market) to house George Yoshio. George Yoshio was becoming 7 months old and now able to stand up in his crib was placed in this sheltered covered trailer while grandfather and grandmother toiled in the fields. Although grandmother intuitively knew if baby George needed anything, his cry would summon her, yet due to her motherly concern for her baby, she would visit with George Yoshio on a periodic thirty minutes intervals. Grandfather would criticize and reprimand grandmother for this unusual attention and her worrisome behavior. Since this was her first born and a male at that, she made up her mind, it was her duty to give this special attention.

Years passed, and in the summer of 1908, grandfather and grandmother were blessed with a new born daughter. They named her Mae Yoshiko. Again, grandfather stated he wanted to give his daughter the Japanese name Yoshiko because it was a derivative of his father's name in Japan. "Yoshio." Grandmother, although out of character relative to the traditional behavior of the Japanese heirarchy, where one does not question the actions of the head of the house, questioned why they needed to name their daughter with the derivative of grandfather's father's name again, since George was named after his father.

Grandmother stated: "I did not question you giving George your father's name, but why do we have to name our daughter after your father?" Grandfather stated: "You be quiet, it is the prerogative of the husband, the head of the household, to make the final decision."

In the Japanese hierarchy of "fu-fu," (husband and wife), husband is dominant, as is in the example of "kun-shin," emperor and subject, emperor is obviously dominant. Therefore, in the typical Japanese social conflict, this is the start of a classical "fu-fu genka" (husband and wife domestic fight). As predicted, grandfather won the shouting match and the daughter was named Mae Yoshiko.

Again, grandmother had to stay home till Mae Yoshiko could be of age so that she could battle the outside environment. Unfortunately, when Mae Yoshiko was old enough to battle the environment, weather changed, the rain started as winter came, and it was mutually agreed that it was not appropriate nor wise to introduce Mae into the cold winter climate.

Another summer had passed, and George Yoshio was becoming of school age, and grandfather and grandmother decided that George needed to start school. Grandfather visited the local school and met with the principal so that he would be well prepared to start school in early September. Meanwhile, Mr. Hamai, grandfather's helper, decided to return to Fukuoka, Japan, so that winter before he left to Japan, the entire community of farmers in the "Trimble Road" area threw a party on a Saturday afternoon in November at the Japanese language/community hall located one half mile north of grandfather's house. George will be quite familiar with this facility shortly, since he will soon will be spending many hours there, attending language school daily, and on Sundays, the Buddhist Sunday School.

What a feast! Grandmother and her women friends made sushi, of all kinds, grandfather went to the San Francisco Bay to fish for striped bass for sashimi, shrimps were boiled, umani, (a vegetable chicken dish) and many other traditional dishes were prepared. The sake flowed profusely, people ate till dawn and grandfather did not get up as early as normal, the next morning; and stated to grandmother, "I think it wouldn't be sacrilegious if they missed one Sunday Buddhist service." It was related by grandmother later, that grandfather had a large hangover on Sunday, and had not been able to sleep soundly the night before.

George started kindergarten that year. Mr. Hamai left grandfather's farm to return to Japan, and George became concerned of his new environment—school. Although he was taken to school on his first day by his father, he was apprehensive on his acceptance and adjustment to his new environment. He soon found out that there were many children of his own ethnic background attending from other farm areas surrounding the school; therefore, adjusted to the new experience very quickly. Grandfather explained to George that he will be picked up around 2:30 p.m. when school ended, and grandfather further stated he wanted to take him on his first day to the language school located near his house, since he felt it was important to introduce George to the Japanese language teacher.

George soon found that his educational endeavors were not a three-quarter day schedule, but soon to be an all day, all week commitment. During the school week, George's schedule was as follows: Monday through Friday, he left at 8:00 a.m. to his regular

English classes and returned home around 3:00 p.m., after 3:00 p.m., he went to his Japanese language school which met during the school week on Monday to Friday from 3:30 p.m. to 5:30 p.m. Language school session also occurred on Saturday mornings. Sunday mornings as usual were allocated for Buddhist Sunday school.

When a Japanese child became of school age attending third grade, it was expected that the child should be able to take care of oneself. The younger brother or sister were more fortunate, since it was understood that the older children had the responsibility for the security and comfort of their younger brothers and sisters.

Japanese Language School

The Japanese language schools were originally formed in the United States to provide the offspring of Isseis born in this country, the knowledge of the Japanese language. This knowledge was necessary and helped facilitate the only means of communication between the parents and children. Prior to instituting these language schools, communications were limited, and at certain times, grievous misunderstandings occurred, due to these language barriers. Further, due to these language barriers, erosion of the unwritten covenant of filial respect to the parents and being loyal to the land were becoming to be in jeopardy. No person could be expected to be a good citizen if he misunderstands his parents or disobey them. The parents of Japanese offspring realized that Japanese language schools afforded the only medium of communication between parents and the child at home, hereby bridging the misunderstandings that could affect family relationships.

The language school had other benefits. Not only did it serve to bridge this communication gap between parent and child, but it served as a place the child could go after he or she was dismissed from public schools. Both father and mother generally were engaged on their farms from dawn till dusk; therefore their concern for their child having "idle mind and time" and falling into bad company was alleviated by the child's language school attendance.

Grandfather and grandmother, the following spring, decided that they should try to farm their (15) acres by themselves after Mr. Hamai left. They rationalized that the only reason they had hired Mr. Hamai was that grandmother had to watch George Yoshio and Mae Yoshiko, limiting grandmother's time in the field. Further, grandfather concluded that he must save some of his money for his children's higher education, and that this might be an opportune time to put away some money not only for their children's college fund, but also money for passage over the Pacific to visit their parents.

Harvest was good that winter and summer, and grandfather and grandmother found at times that they were short of hands for the harvest of certain crops. The good neighbors who were also farmers gave them a hand since many farmers who started their farms prior to grandfather and grandmother's arrival in America had offspring older of age than George and Mae. They were a great help not only for their family, but to their neighbors.

George completed high school in 1922, four years after the end of World War I, and was getting ready for college. He excelled in his class, and became the class salutatorian, which made grandfather and grandmother exceptionally proud parents, having a scholar who was destined for great things. All their friends in the "Trimble Road" area came to his commencement exercises, and later grandfather and grandmother had a party at their home to honor George. It was reported that the party went on past midnight. Grandfather did not get up very early again the next day, for his alcohol consumption might have been greater than at the party that was held for Mr. Hamai's departure to Japan. Grandfather and grandmother were the happiest, proudest parents of the farming community of Trimble Road. Their son had graduated at near top of his class, their daughter Mae was also being acclaimed as the brightest person in the third grade class and farming was prospering.

Then suddenly, shock and confusion reigned at the "Trimble Road" area. George got sick without any warning and it was predicted that the seriousness and the rarity of his disease made recovery a slim chance. A few weeks passed and George's condition got worse and within the third week he passed on. George's parents were in complete shock, wondering where justice was! Grandfather who was a strong person, who never had shown emotion outward, since he was schooled at an early boyhood that it was not manly to show one's emotion and in fact it is a sign of weakness, cried profusely hearing of his son's death and stated:

"Why? Why?"

A wake was held at the San Jose Buddhist Church conducted by then Reverends Takahashi and Sasaki. All the farmers and their families attended the wake, including all the families from Fukuoka prefecture, and the many other friends of grandfather and grandmother. The church was overflowing, people had to congregate outdoors, and it had rained the night before, thus grandfather and grandmother became quite concerned for the parishoners who came to give their last respects. Hundreds of Japanese passed by the still form of George and included in this procession were George's high school classmates, the principal of the school and most of his teachers. After the service, the attendees to the wake visited grandfather and grandmother's home to give their last respects prior to the final services at the cemetery. The next day the final funeral was held, again, the family wept, but all agreed, "they must carry on."

Koden

In times of need, such as funerals and death, the entire Japanese community usually attended funeral services for those who had passed on. In attending, koden is offered to the deceased families in form of certain amount of monies in a sealed envelope with clear name and address of the donor. This act is repeated for each funeral and it is incumbent on the deceased family to return the exact or greater amount received to the donor's family when tragedy strikes. In order to make certain that monies are returned after the passing of one's friends, or relatives, a record is kept of each donor listing the exact amount received from the previous funeral. When any Japanese death was announced in the newspapers, each family referred to their own records to make certain (if koden is received), then the exact amount of monies previously received or more were placed in a sealed envelope and brought to the funeral. This method of giving, reduced the normal financial burden of a costly funeral. Again, this form of giving mutual self-help all tended to create a strong bond between all Japanese indefinitely, creating further isolation of this ethnic group from the total community.

Festivals

Besides crisis such as funerals and happy occasions such as weddings, certain occasions became important times where the family came together as extended families, for example as Bon and New Year.

One of the most important holiday from a religious standpoint is Bon. Bon season occurs in July. This is a solemn time where memorial services are held giving thanks and remembrance and appreciation to the past ancestors and loved ones. This was a special Bon for the Koga family. This was the first Bon, (Hatsu bon), of the passing away of George Yoshio. Grandfather, grandmother and daughter Mae Yoshiko, all attended the special memorial service wearing their best attire. Following the service, Bon Dance was held with the participation of males and females dressed in happi coats and kimonos, respectively. Mae Yoshiko—clad in a colorful kimono performed in the Bon Dance, expressing joy that their loved ones have reached the promised land of Nirvana. One person in the crowd during this festival was whispering: "Isn't that Mr. Koga? He is certainly the most distinguished and well-dressed gentleman at the Bon?" Her friend agreed!

The other important holiday in Japan, is New Year. This was not a particular happy year for the Koga family, since they had lost their son, and were still mourning his death. Yet, grandfather, being a sensitive, yet a pragmatic person, agreed with the family that a great tragedy had occurred, but stated: "Life must go on."

New Year celebrations lasts on the farm usually two weeks, and it is a time when farmers exchange gifts and banquets are given, Usually, the husband's family visits his relatives initially, and after that is completed, visits to his wife's relatives are initiated. Visits are usually done by the male members of the family, since the women members are busily preparing and serving guests that visit their homes. During these festive times, great quantities of food are prepared prior to New Year, and as the celebration continues, food are replenished by the women members of the family. Therefore, during this period of time, the female members of the family are either cooking or serving the male visitors. The relatives and friends, by tradition and custom, brought gifts on this occasion, such as sacks of rice, gallons of shoyu, or sake.

Grandfather, receiving these gifts, would display them in the parlor. As a boy growing up, seeing the sacks of rice stacked to the ceiling, one wondered if the floor would cave in. Fortunately, the rice and other supplies were consumed in a short time, giving relief to the fragile floor.

Chapter 3
THE FIRST AMERICANS

The Nisei

Nisei, born of Japanese immigrant parents soon realized that tensions were developing between the Issei parents' "Japanese Way" and the newly found "American Way." The Nisei found he or she could mingle more freely than their parents with other races and ate American as well as Japanese foods. He or she was bilingual due to the insistence of the Issei parents to attend Japanese language schools and became somewhat socially frustrated on what alternative life styles one should explore.

The Isseis' expectation that their children should perpetuate traditional institutions, values and customs of the "Japanese Way of Life" began to somewhat erode, due to these outside associations and contacts. The Niseis' outside experiences differed and moved away from the close tight knit Japanese community the Isseis had created for themselves, started to worry the Isseis. The Issei's sense of being wholly "Japanese" no longer was possible due to these outside influences, and the family system, the "ie", the role of the patriarch and the role of each member and community obligations, was now becoming candidate for modifications. This became very upsetting to the first generation immigrants, the Isseis.

Pattern of life during the early 1900's to around 1920's, although changing, had minimal effect on the total family and social structure, because the Nisei, would not experiment with his or her new found multi-faceted social environment, culturally did not take a "giant step", and would not "take a chance" that might cause him or her to fail in his/her new environment.

After the 1920's, when a large majority of Niseis started high school and eventually were attending college, the matured Nisei, having contact with a broader spectrum of society and associating with different backgrounds and cultures, became less comfortable with traditional familial and social behaviors as originally dictated by their parents. A conflict of generations was becoming increasingly inevitable.

This generational conflict between the Issei and the Nisei during the 1920's and 1930's is outlined by Misako Yamamoto, "Cultural Conflicts and Accommodations of the First and Second Generation Japanese." Yamamoto, depicts that the Nisei generation as an adolescent population comprised of youngsters under the age of eighteen. After many years in the United States, isolated in their own rural Japanese community, the Isseis were confortable in their rural "ie" pattern of Japanese culture, language and values. The Isseis' expectations were to have their offspring, the Niseis retain and carry on the many traditional patterns they had brought from their homeland.

The Issei parents argued: You are foremost Japanese and even though implanted in America, you must maintain Japanese values of filial piety, obligation to community and authority (on), reciprocal obligation (giri), a fatalistic acceptance of unforseen circumstances in life (shikata-ga-nai) and a fear of shame (haji). Further, education was highly valued and hard work, perserverance and frugality were encouraged.

Shortly after graduation from high school in Hawaii, the fourth son of Mitsuhei and Mura Tanaka, Richard in 1920, joined the United States Navy. How proud he was! He related that he was the only Nisei on his ship. Joining the Navy had a traumatic effect on the parents of Richard I. Tanaka because his parents knew by this action they were going to lose, very soon, their favorite son. He was picked to be the brightest and most inventive son of the family who had excelled in high school and would for certain make a good student at the university. Yet, due to his urge to explore, and stating many times to his parents that there are many parts of this world one must explore to enrich one's mind and learn the wonders of the entire world, he went on to seek his adventure. "Join the Navy and see the world!" What a challenge—My father as part of the first tour of duty landed in San Francisco from Pearl Harbor, Oahu, Hawaii, and fell in love with San Francisco and visited Santa Clara Valley, "The Valley of Heart's Delight."

After many visits to San Francisco and with the completion of his tour of duty, he returned to San Francisco, and was discharged in 1924. He found a job at the San Francisco Produce Market and after two years of employment at the Produce Market, he decided to try his fortune in the Santa Clara Valley. My father was an ambitious man. Realizing that he could make his fortune in buying and transporting the farmers' produce to San Francisco, he proceeded immediately into putting a down payment on a truck from the limited savings of the Navy tour and the two years of employment at the produce market. Later, he extended his produce transportation business to include Los Angeles. Father soon became well-known for his fairness and attention he gave to his farmers' accounts.

In the June of 1925, Mae Yoshiko Koga, graduated with great distinction from high school and stated that she would like to go to college and eventually become a medical doctor. My mother had made up her mind regarding her career, because she wanted to go into medical research to identify certain diseases that were still a mystery to the world. My mother had been greatly affected by the tragic and sudden death of her brother and said on many occasions during her childhood that she desired the opportunity to continue her studies to do medical research.

Farming in the years immediately before 1926 was not exceptionally profitable, and farmers anticipating higher yields and greater labor savings by mechanization got into heavy debt. My mother's parents were no exception. They had placed all their savings of the past 20 years which had been saved for George's college education and a future visit back to Japan into tractors, plows, culivators, seeders and a new barn to house these equipment. Prince, the farm horse, was getting old and was being retired to live in leisure. The new farm equipment was soon expected to show dividends of saving labor and grandfather was happy that if savings could be realized from the farm his daughter could go to college and become a doctor, her life long desire.

In 1926, mother enrolled at San Jose Normal College, and found college both challenging and exciting. Time went by quickly and being exceptionally bright, she had no problem attending school and helping out on the farm occasionally. However, due to short-handedness on the farm and falling farm prices, mother in her sophomore year in college had to withdraw from college to help on the farm.

Baishakunin

Marriage is one of the most important event in lives of all mankind. Traditionally, it is a Japanese custom, that parents are expected to pick a bride for their son. In the case of father, since he was here in California alone, he requested a mutual couple that the Koga family knew to be the "baishakunin," or "go between," who made all the arrangements for the marriage. Outsiders view this arrangement a forced marriage, or arrangement devoid of consent from both parties. This is not so, since both parties have the perfect right for refusal prior to the announcement of betrothal. Marriages of Niseis in later years would not be subscribing to the past Japanese philosophy that "love is not essential before marriage, but something which comes after marriage." Therefore, "baishakunin" will become only a formality in future marriages, and marriages will be consummated only because the essence of love exists between the two parties.

Wedding

Richard and Mae Tanaka's wedding in 1928 was the largest social event of the year. Farmers from the "Trimble Road" area were all invited as well as town folks and people from San Francisco as well as Los Angeles. Grandfather and grandmother borrowed monies from friends to make this a memorable event. The wedding was held at the San Jose Buddhist Church Temple and the overflowing crowd on the covered veranda (engawa) tolerated and unusual early summer heat, viewed the wedding ceremony being performed through the windows. As usual, people outside, were conversing in a whisper, but later started to talk in higher than normal decibel and soon the bothersome conversation entered the quiet and solemn temple. One of the ushers had to return outside of the church and scold the guests standing on the surrounding veranda to be quiet. Embarrassed, the guests kept their conversation or remarks to minimum until the wedding ceremony was over.

At the reception, traditional Japanese cultural singing were performed honoring the wedding, guests consuming a great content of alcohol and without inhibition of any kind, got up and sang familiar colloquial folk songs of their region of Japan, and due to the size of the crowd, the reception although having started at 6:00 p.m., was still going on after 11:00 p.m. By 12:00 a.m., needless to say, the party ended, and the young married couple stayed at the local boarding house that night, prior to leaving on their honeymoon. After three weeks of honeymooning which took them throughout California, my parents settled down to help manage my grandfather and grandmother's farm. In the spring of 1928, prior to the marriage of my father and mother, the prices of the New York Stock Exchange was showing signs of reaching its historic high, and farmers without any awareness of the seriousness of the shaky economy and not having any sophistication to predict future results of this strong surge were placed in a position where they did not know how to protect themselves of their finances. A mania for speculation swept the country, and thousands of small investors having placed their entire savings in common stocks soon found that the great depression was here as the market crashed on October 29, 1929.

The Great Depression was a worldwide phenomenon caused by the economic inbalances resulting from industrialization and the chaos of the Great War. Everyone was affected by the depression especially the small investors and farmers such as my grandfather who had had a large loan to finance his own mechanization program. Farming prices tumbled, people in great hordes were out of jobs and were standing in soup lines. In a few years, mother would reflect that she did not have the opportunity to graduate from college due to this Great Depression and its impact on finances. Now, realizing the financial jeopardy of the Koga and the Tanaka families were at stake, all of the members of the respective families started to seriously concentrate on effects to bridge this major crisis.

In late summer of 1930, a daughter, June, was born and following her birth, son, Richard, was born in 1931.

My mother was a strong person both mentally and physically. She had to be for she had the responsibility to the tending for her offspring which included feeding, bathing and comforting them

51

in their childhood and if time permitted, occasionally talked and played with them.

On the farm, most mothers never had time to themselves or had even time to sleep. The normal day for a mother on the rural farm would be to rise before 5:00 a.m., start the fire of the wood or coal in the stove and prepare breakfast for the other members of the family. If she had young offspring, she was up prior to this, to heat the evaporated "Pet" milk for the baby's formula. She would make breakfast usually for grandfather, then her husband, then her children. The grandmother usually would help with the chores of making breakfast and later the washing of the dishes. After all the members of the family had completed their breakfast, the mother and grandmother and the baby ate their breakfast.

Their typical menu was to make do with the toasts that were left and cold or extra eggs and bacon that was cooked but not eaten on the particular morning. Grandmother would complain that the coffee, eggs and toast were cold, since it may have been sitting on the table for a hour or more after it has been cooked.

After breakfast, baby's clothes and diapers were washed and hung out to dry. The other members's clothes were usually left to be washed on Saturdays, when more time was available, since all farmers took this day off, because produce markets were closed on Sundays.

When breakfast and some of the general cleanup of the house were completed, the "bento" (Japanese food placed in a wooden box) for lunch was prepared. Then mother hurriedly left for the fields.

Grandmother normally stayed home to tend to the small ones. There was a practical reason for grandmother to tend and watch over the baby who could not care for one's self. The mother of the baby was obviously younger, stronger and more energetic and could do heavier chores and had greater stamina then the usually older grandmother. Therefore, she would be a greater asset in the fields. Production was important. Many farms during this time, could not afford outside help, therefore father's 12-to-14-hour day, six-days-a-week schedule became a normal routine, rather than an exception in running a truck farm.

For a rural farmer's child growing up in this era, Saturday afternoons were the most joyous times. It was a time allocated to visit with one's parents. The parents were usually home doing household chores. Mother cleaned, laundered and mended clothes, while father usually repaired the many items, that he had no time for, as he needed all available time to tend the fields during the week.

My father had to do many chores around the house, such as patching the roof in anticipation of early winter or fixing a leak in the trough that was used to wash his vegetables during the week. As a child, I followed his every step, observing his wide and varied knowledge for the repairing refrigerators, to tuning of cars, to carpentry, all suggesting to me that this is a man with infinite knowledge, and truly a remarkable man. How he acquired such a vast knowledge, still amazes me!

He had learned in early life that all things had interdependencies, and therefore, valued life. Life of all forms, I remember being told, is important. My mother had related to the children that father stated he must build a barn for "Prince," our horse, who was retired after the purchase of the tractors and trucks.

He rationalized that our horse had been an integral part of our family, and we were completely dependent upon him for our own livelihood. We depended on this animal to plow, cultivate and pull our trailer that brought the produce to the vegetable storage and platform area. My father would further comment that the horse provided all the children the opportunity to ride him and generally created a happy atmosphere for all. In later years, the lean-to that housed the horse was removed and a magnificent two story barn was erected, housing a hay loft above the stable area for "Prince."

When New Year came, it was customary and a tradition to pound special steamed rice to make mochi (rice cake) shaped to be round on the sides and flat top and bottom so that two or three mochis could be stacked on top of each other. My father would never forgot to place the ceremonial "good luck" stacked mochis in the barn symbolizing the honor and longevity for our horse.

I could vividly recall my mother telling the children, when work was done that Prince would be unharnessed by grandfather Koga, and either mom or her brother of our age would ride him or let him run or gallop to his favorite area, the stable near our house.

As my mother was expecting another child and my sister and I were becoming older, my father decided that we children should have more space and have separate rooms. My father, an experienced carpenter, designed and added one additional room to our original three bedroom house.

I still remember how proud we were of father for building this new addition to our home. Our home was located off a long road off of Trimble Road in San Jose, California, rectangular in shape with a wood shingled gabled roof. It had one large area for a kitchen, dining and living area and off of the living room were three bedroom prior to this addition. One room was for my grandfather and grandmother, another for my mother and father and third room was shared originally with my sister, and later became my older sister's room. My sister slept in this room by herself, until my younger sister, Barbara, was born in December, 1940. How proud I was that father gave me the newly added bedroom.

Chapter 4
ONE'S ALLEGIANCE AND LOYALTY

Hawaii

As the Japanese troops invaded Manchuria, the Hawaiian press and radio recited through editorials concerns of Japan's energetic expansion program in Asia and their possible profound effect on the "Islands."

"The political-military web around Manchuria is so vast, so complicated, so woven of ancient as well as latter-day issues," editorialized the Honolulu Star Bulletin, "that judgment on the rights and wrongs of the situation is difficult. But its signficance is plain—an ordered and tremendously powerful move by Japan to extend her "sphere of influence" in highly important and strategic territory."[8]

These persuasive and far reaching editorials gave rise for the question whether the immigrants having Japanese names living in Hawaii from 1872 to the 1940's were suspects.

Suspicions were raised:

1. Why did the majority contingency of Japanese in Hawaii live on the coastline?

2. If Japanese Issei and Nisei were loyal American citizens, why do they persist in maintaining language school and Buddhist temples?

3. They cannot be trusted, since they do not participate with the total society, they isolate themselves, identifying only with their ethnic community.

4. What secret organizations are they members of, having strange sounding names such as kenjin-kai, fujin-kai, ni-honjin-kai, etc.

The press and radio further advanced the theory, that it must be a reality that the Japanese immigrants and their children must be the advance fifth column movement that were brought to Hawaii to undermine the internal security before the invasion. These are trained spies, saboteurs and agents of the emperor and his war lords. The public should question their allegiance: "Why did the Japanese immigrants in Hawaii before World War II remain of Japanese citizens, subject to Japanese laws and military draft? The only reason they maintained this legal status as Japanese citizens, must be because they desired to keep close ties, allegiance and contact with their homeland."

This public erroneous unfounded perception grew from the fact that by American law during this era, Japanese aliens were barred from becoming naturalized citizens. This act was revised in latter years, yet most Americans during this time did not know such a law existed.

With these negative questions and comments from the press, radio and public, relocation of Japanese immigrants and their children of Hawaii after the bombing of Pearl Harbor seem to be a rational decision. Yet, only few isolated Japanese immigrants and citizens of Hawaii were imprisoned or relocated into relocation or internment camps. Shouldn't they be listed as more than suspicious, after the devastating bombing of Pearl Harbor by the Japanese?

California

Japanese in Hawaii, although being self-reliant individuals with close ties with their ethnic communities became more involved with the greater communities in their cities and locales, while the Japanese in California due to their isolationist pattern were painted with fabricated negative images and comments by the jealous less productive agriculturalists and horticulturists. The public was told that the Japanese were a menace, agents to their motherland and never could be trusted. Why do they desire to stick with "their own kind only?"

These propaganda campaigns questioning their character, loyalty and allegiance to America were advanced from the inception of the Japanese immigration starting in 1868. Organizations in California, such as the American Legion, Daughters of the Golden West, and the Native Sons active and supportive in the passage of the 1924 immigration law barring Japanese travel to the United States, were the first to join forces with the agricultural interests who saw landholding, agricultural output and quality products as a competitive threat. They gave an enthusiastic support for the complete removal of Japanese and Japanese-American citizens from the West Coast.

Hysteria during the war played into the hands of the racist agriculturists. They played on false patriotism, on suspicion, on the isolationism of the Japanese from the greater society and community, all giving credence that they are surely agents of Emperor Hirohito, and if they don't stop this menace, it will be the beginning of the end of America.

The racists continued: "Further, removal, incarceration, relocation out of California will be a generous effort of the United States government. How can we protect the Isseis and Niseis, if one's son is killed by a Japanese. Enraged whites will seek the local Japanese and get revenge, for a "Jap is a Jap!" How can we protect the Japanese from the Filipinos in California, if they hear of the atrocities committed on their homeland? And what if a Japanese home is bombed?"

Aside from the advanced thesis of protection of the Japanese from the enraged populace, the racists raised the same questions and doubts addressed on Japanese in Hawaii:

1. California has a large coastline and many Japanese in California live near the ocean, therefore must be agents of the Emperor of Japan.
2. They cannot be trusted, for they join secret organizations and the Isseis are still citizens of Japan.

Therefore, assessing the military threat and the so-called "humanitarian reasons" for the preservation of their lives, various groups, organizations, lobbyists and policymakers all joined together to fabricate the "military and public necessity" to remove 120,000 Japanese and Japanese-American citizens from the West Coast, which included the states of Washington, Oregon, California and parts of Arizona.

On February 19, 1942, President Franklin D. Roosevelt signed Executive Order 9066, which gave authority to the Secretary of War or any military commander designated by the Secretary of War to create military areas to exclude any and all persons from the designated areas.

On March 3, 1942, Lieutenant General John DeWitt, military commander of the West Coast, directed all Japanese whether alien or citizens evacuated to so called "relocation camps", which were actually barbed wired, military guarded concentration camps.

The total number that were relocated from the West Coast numbered more than 120,000 men, women and children. Herded into crowded trains, allowed to carry one suitcase of belongings these "quiet brave Americans" traveled in congested tightly confined trains to internment camps with innocuous picturesque names like Tule Lake, Heart Mountain, Manzanar, Poston, Gila River, all scattered in arid or cold barren wastes of the continental United States. Young and old often died prior to reaching their destination, due to the lack of food and water during the long travel; yet most of these hearty, obedient citizens survived to become "better Americans in a greater America."

"Military and Humanitarian Necessity"

Most historians, social scientists and legal practioners all are in agreement today, that the wholesale removal of Japanese from the West Coast had no foundation and denied the personal rights of American citizens guaranteed under the United States Constitution. Further, no evidence or credence was established for the need for their removal due to "military and humanitarian necessities."

If "military necessity" was paramount, why weren't Japanese in Hawaii removed? Had not Japan, the "mother country" attacked the continental United States by bombing Pearl Harbor? If distrust was paramount, shouldn't the Japanese in Hawaii be removed immediately after the bombing? Wouldn't it be rational that after Japan attacked Pearl Harbor she would set up a military base especially after such a devastating destruction and crippling of Pearl Harbor? Wouldn't it seem logical that there must have been Japanese agents either planted or existing in Honolulu, if in fact, Japan was able to destroy the harbor with little or no resistance? Agents must have been installed and became part of the military, since there were no warnings of the attack?

These questions of loyalty were raised by the public, media and the military, and although being somewhat convincing and racist in nature, the self-serving elements during this time were not in the majority in Hawaii. If only some of these concerns raised were factual, why weren't Hawaii's Japanese incarcerated into concentration camps? If for no other reason, as argued by the proponents for incarceration of the West Coast Japanese, by securing and excluding of Hawaii's Japanese, it would afford at least, protection of the Japanese from the public and will further insure the protection of vital United States military installations and industries. If it is logical to incarcerate West Coast Japanese on security and military necessities, there seems to be ample grounds for detention of Hawaii's Japanese.

Yet, Hawaii's Japanese, seemingly more threatening than the West Coast's Japanese were not incarcerated in mass, and only 3,250 persons including ("voluntary") internees or approximately 2% of the population were excluded.

In Hawaii, the Japanese labor force was vital and necessary to run the shipyards and other defense installations. Therefore, if the Hawaii's Japanese were incarcerated, and sent to concentration camps, it was reasoned by the military, that those very defense installations that were bombed by the same perceived "Japanese" on the Islands would have to close and become inoperative. What a strange dichotomy! First, the Japanese in Hawaii are being accused that they can't be trusted, that their loyalty was questionable, yet became the main force in keeping the shipyards open, and U.S. ships afloat.

Another important circumstance, unlike the West Coast Japanese, was that Hawaii's Japanese were not heavily involved in commerce or agriculture, thus proved to be no threat to the economy controlled by large "white" corporations. Therefore, farmers and other entrepreneurs did not come forward to argue for their exclusion.

Finally, the military stepped forward and defended Hawaii's Japanese. After extensive investigation and their importance relative to the total labor force, the military concluded that the question of loyalty, security, trust of protection for Japanese may be of some concern, yet inconsequential in nature.

Thus, the issue of loyalty and security was resolved in Hawaii by the Army, Navy and British intelligence agencies. One such study by Curtis Munson, a government agent, who had completed an extensive investigation on the West Coast Japanese population concluded that the Japanese in Hawaii were closely attached to the Islands. He reported that although Japanese in Hawaii were not particularly loyal to America, they would do nothing to endanger their island home.

"The consensus of opinion is that there will be no racial uprising of the Japanese in Honolulu . . . it may be well to state here in a general way that everyone . . . places loyalty to Hawaii first, and the United States, second. This is not meant to impugn their loyalty—but they love the Islands."[9]

Munson concluded that ninety-eight percent of the Nisei were loyal American citizens and only two percent may be possible disloyal and should be removed from Hawaii; incarcerated in prisons or sent to relocation camps in the West Coast. Munson further stated: "Nisei" were "bright young things," and concluded the only concern was a racial uprising between Filipinos and Japanese and concluded that treasonous actions among Japanese were not expected and "the big majority anyhow would be neutral or even actively loyal."[10]

Despite the affirmation by the military that the Japanese in Hawaii were basically loyal to Hawaii and the United States, proponents for the removal of Japanese were being encouraged.

Albert J. Horlings, in his July 25, 1942 article in "The Nation," questioned the conclusions of the military of the Japanese being loyal, trustworthy and having no allegiance to Japan by arguing that if the United States government finds indisputable national and military necessity for the removal of West Coast Japanese and suspension of their constitutional rights, then Hawaii's 150,000 Japanese should be evacuated, since they were of even greater risk. Horlings added: "to a remarkable degree Hawaii's Japanese are untouched by American ways; all their pride of race family and religion binds them to Japan. Thousands see or hear almost nothing American, while they consume Japanese food, Japanese clothing, Japanese music, Japanese pictures, Japanese newspapers and magazines by the shipload." Horlings concluded that the victory of the Rising Sun over the Islands would be most welcome by the Island Japanese.

Thomas Ige, a Japanese-American, wrote a letter to "The Nation," rebutting Horling's article, "Hawaii's 150,000 Japanese", argued that Horlings totally misread the spirit and allegiance of Hawaii's Japanese-Americans. If Hawaii was attacked, the overwhelming majority of Hawaii's Japanese-Americans will fight and stand by America. Ige's exemporary remarks were echoed throughout Hawaii and rationality prevailed.

Although 120,000 Japanese were removed from the West Coast, Hawaii's Japanese, comprising thirty-seven percent of the population were not evacuated from the most strategic vulnerable military installation (Pearl Harbor), since the military concluded that they were necessary and needed to provide the essential labor force to carry on the war efforts. It is now clear that Japanese in Hawaii had established firm loyalties and associations with the non-Japanese population who championed their cause. Their positive posture in the greater community aided their plight for reason and fairness. This loyalty and bond of friendship of the non-white community became a strong public voice to affirm that the Island's Japanese were loyal to Hawaii and the United States.

In contrast, Mainland's Japanese, smaller in population in relationship to the total population of the West Coast, resided in small rural areas isolated from the greater community. Very few whites had been in contact with the Japanese on the West Coast, and it is known that organized racial campaign was initiated as early as 1868, when the first immigrants , the Wakamatsu Tea Colony were established in the Gold Country near Auburn, California.

The Japanese on the West Coast were perceived to be secretive isolationists. Yet, the Japanese in the spirit of "getting along," appeasing racial slurs from some, not wanting to be in conflict roles with their white counterparts and the community, being non visible and non existant, all fortified the perception that these immigrants must have had ulterior motives by these secretive actions. This isolationist policy of Mainland's Japanese, and his/her assumption that by not becoming involved with the total community, avoiding competition or confrontation, he/she might be perceived as a superior citizen and neighbor in one's new found land, became his/her downfall.

As history now relates, this isolation from the greater community was one of the major reasons why very few championed the tragic plight or the affirmation that the Japanese on the West Coast were loyal and trustworthy citizens as confirmed by the citizenry for Hawaii's Japanese. Therefore, propaganda for military necessity and the hate hysteria created fuel for the ultimate removal of 120,000 Japanese and Japanese-Americans from the West Coast of the United States without the constitutional guarantee of "due process."

Japanese-American Citizens League

In order to create greater visibility for the West Coast Japanese, an organization called the Japanese-American Citizens League (JACL) was formed in 1920. It was not until 1941, under the agressive leadership of Mike Masaoka that this organization began to have national status. Although (JACL) had peripheral support from some churches, the American Civil Liberties Union (ACLU), and the National Association for the Advancement of Colored People (NAACP), the Japanese and this organization could not exert any political "clout" to counteract the local, state and national governments as well as the racists and agriculturalists who started their Japanese exclusion campaign in the late 1860's.

Prior to the declaration of War by Congress, the bombing by the Japanese on Pearl Harbor on December 7, 1941 and Roosevelt's unjust Executive Order 9066 excluding Japanese from the West Coast, Mike Masaoka read to the United States Senate and printed in the Congressional Record on May 9, 1941, the (JACL) Creed which describes the feelings and the positive attitude of Japanese-Americans during that era toward America:

JACL Creed

I am proud that I am an American citizen of Japanese ancestry, for my very background makes me appreciate more fully the wonderful advantages of this nation. I believe in her institutions, ideals and traditions; I glory in her heritage; I boast of her history; I trust in her future. She has granted me liberties and opportunities such as no individual enjoys in this world today. She has given me an education befitting kings. She has entrusted me to build a home, to earn a livelihood, to worship, think, speak, and act as I please—as a free man equal to every other man.

Although some individuals may discriminate against me, I shall never become bitter or lose faith, for I know that such persons are not representative of the majority of the American people. True, I shall do all in my power to discourage such practices, but I shall do in the American way: aboveboard, in the open, through courts of law, by education, by proving myself to be worthy of equal treatment and consideration. I am firm in my belief that American sportsmanship and attitude of fair play will judge citizenship and patriotism on the basis of action and achievement, and not on the basis of physical characteristics. Because I believe in America, and I trust she believes in me, I pledge myself to do her honor to her at all times and in all places; to support her constitution; to obey her laws; to respect her flag; to defend her against all enemies; foreign or domestic; to actively assume my duties and obligations as a citizen, cheerfully and without any reservations whatsoever, in the hope that I may become a better American in a greater America.

Chapter 5
VOLUNTARY EXODUS

Pearl Harbor

After the bombing of Pearl Harbor on December 7, 1941 by Japanese airplanes, my father became concerned for not only the security of the family, but also the possible separation of the family, especially my grandfather. Grandfather served in leadership roles at the local Buddhist Church as well as the Fukuoka Kenjinkai, Nihonjinkai and other ethnic oriented organizations.

On December 8, 1942, President Roosevelt addressed a joint session of Congress expressing the outrage, shock and damage caused by the "sneak attack" of the Japanese, and noted that this day will serve as a day of infamy. The President on that day requested and received a declaration of war against Japan, and on December 11, 1941, the United States declared war on Italy and Germany.

After the bombing of Pearl Harbor, the Federal Bureau of Investigation (FBI), on December 8, 1941, was mobilized and given the authority to detain enemy aliens and confiscate enemy property wherever found. This authority was obtained from President Roosevelt by his signing of Proclamation 2525, pursuant to the Alien Act of 1798. The FBI drew up categories of aliens to be arrested under this Proclamation. Category "A": Aliens who led cultural or assistance organizations; category "B": slightly less suspicious aliens; and category "C": members of those who donated to ethnic groups, Japanese language teachers and Buddhist clergy. With these categories, it affected most older Japanese and Japanese-Americans.

By December 10, 1942, FBI Director J. Edgar Hoover announced that "practically all" whom he initially planned to arrest through his extensive investigation had been arrested. In his custody, he reported that 1,291 Japanese, (397 in Hawaii), 924 in the continental United States, 887 Germans, 147 Italians were being detained.

After hearing about many of my grandfather's friends being arrested by the FBI, and placed in custody, my father became very concerned for the possible separation and security of our family. Racism was being advanced by the public without restraint, and certain questionable arrests by the FBI were being made. Will grandfather be next? Grandfather being in leadership role with the local Buddhist Church and many ethnic organizations was a prime target for the FBI. Therefore, my father's concern for the family was real. Phrases like "Good Jap is a dead Jap," "A Jap is a Jap," and "Get rid of all Japs," were common phrases that were used, fueled by hysteria of that time. Although unfounded arrests were exercised, no one effectively stood up to resist these orchestrated unjust actions.

Due to these known unannounced FBI raids, my father and grandfather inventoried all of the so-called contraband in our house, collected them and systematically dumped it into our outdoor latrine. After removing and dumping the contraband, foreign magazines, newspapers and even Japanese art objects (except a small Buddhist shrine "obutsudan"), my father made plans to leave San Jose for the Military Zone 2, which at that time was noted as a "white zone" area, protected and not destined for evacuation. This directive would be rescinded at a latter date and be removed fom the protective area due to "military necessity."

My father hurriedly called Mr. Hara, a good family friend in Dinuba, located in Central California (Military Zone 2) and asked if we could stay at their home till we could build or find a home in that area. Mr. Hara enthusiastically stated: "Come on down, sure stay with us as long as possible, and if you want to build a home, build it on our property and in that way, you will have a rent free home." Father commented to Mr. Hara, what a great friend he was, very helpful and always showing great kindness throughout the many years of association with our family. With gratitude, father thanked him for his generous offer.

Now arrangements started to be made to dispose of the crops, farm equipment, furniture and other tangible items not necessary for our trip or livelihood in Dinuba. Father impressed on mother and the rest of the family that we must leave as soon as possible since he knew grandfather will be visited by the FBI, because of his leadership role on many of the Japanese organizations and the church. As anticipated, in January of 1942, we were visited by the FBI and grandfather was interrogated. The FBI, looked through our house, barn and other out buildings, and although finding no contraband, Japanese art objects or publications, took grandfather into custody, but later released him after one day of detention.

After grandfather's release my father stated: "We must leave as soon as possible," since he heard that other Japanese Isseis' who were also brought into custody and released had been rearrested. "It is imperative we must dispose of our crops, equipment and furniture immediately, for the sake of our family we will take a loss and leave." "We must, we must."

Meanwhile, Congressman Ford, columnist Henry McLemore and General DeWitt, all were advancing various reasons for the exclusions of Japanese such as native-born Japanese, should voluntarily placed themselves in concentration camps if they are truly loyal; or that Japanese are a threat to our security; and that Nisei born in the United States are the most disloyal of all Japanese.

Further, J. Edgar Hoover, Director of the FBI, sent the attorney general his analysis of the mass exclusion and his opposition to DeWitt's fabricated, personal, biased opinions. Director Hoover commented:

"The necessity for mass evacuation is based primarily upon public and political pressure rather than on factual data. Public hysteria and in some instances, the comments of the press and radio announcers, have resulted in a tremendous amount of pressure being brought to bear on Governor Olson and Earl Warren, Attorney General of the State, and on the military authorities. . .

Local officials, press and citizens have started widespread movement demanding complete evacuation of all Japanese citizens and alien alike."[11]

Supporting Congressman Ford, columnist McLemore and General DeWitt's thesis for the exclusion of Japanese from California, were numerous organizations. Organizations such as the Native Sons and the Daughters of the Golden West, saw the Japanese as threat to the security of the United States.

"Had the warnings been heeded—had the federal and state authorities been "on the alert" and rigidly enforced the Exclusion Law and the Alien Land Law; had the Jap propaganda agencies in this country been silenced; had the legislation been enacted . . . denying citizenship to offspring of all aliens ineligible to citizenship; had the Japs been prohibited from colonizing in strategic locations; had not Jap-dollars been so eagerly sought by white landowners and businessmen; had a dull ear been turned to the honeyed words of the Japs and the pro-Japs; had the yellow-Jap and the white-Jap "fifth columnists" been disposed of within the law; had Japan been denied the privilege of using California as a breeding ground for dual-citizens (Nisei)— the treacherous Japs probably would not have attacked Pearl Harbor on December 7, 1941, and this country could not today be at war with Japan."[12]

During this time on the same day my grandfather was arrested by the FBI on January 16, 1942, in Washington, West Coast congressmen and senators began reciting identical scenarios. Congressman Ford of Los Angeles took the lead by stating that his California mail was running heavily in favor of exclusion and internment of Japanese:

"I knew that there will be some complications in connection with a matter like this, particularly where there are native born Japanese, who are citizens. My suggestions in connection with this area as follows:
  1. That these native born Japanese either are or are not loyal to the United States.

67

2. That all Japanese, whether citizens or not, be placed
   in inland concentration camps. As justification for this,
   I submit that if an American born Japanese, who is a
   citizen, is really patriotic and wishes to make his con-
   tribution to the safety and welfare of this country, right
   here is his opportunity to do so, namely, that by permitting himself to be placed in a concentration camp,
   he would be making his sacrifice and he should be willing to do it if he is patriotic and is working for us. As
   against his sacrifice, millions of other native born citizens are willing to lay down their lives, which is far
   greater sacrifice, of course, than being placed in concentration camp.[13]

The sentiments of fear and anger for the easy strike on Pearl
Harbor and the initial systematic victories in the Far East by the
Japanese, created even in the minds of the so-called "fair and
rational" newspaper writers, a sense of irrationality and in a
spirit of psuedo-patriotism, infused race hatred and war hysteria
in their commentaries.

Henry McLemore, a Hearst syndicated columnist, published a
vicious diatribe:

The only Japanese apprehended have been the ones the
FBI actually had something on. The rest of them, so help
me, are free as birds. There isn't an airport in California
that isn't flanked by Japanese farms. There is hardly an air
field where the same situation doesn't exist. . .

I know this is the melting pot of the world and all men
are created equal and there just be no such thing as race or
creed hatred, but do those things go when a country is fighting for its life? Not in my book. No country has ever won a
war because of courtesy and I trust and pray we won't be
the first because of the lovely, gracious spirit. . .

I am for immediate removal of every Japanese on the West
Coast to a point deep in the interior. I don't mean a nice part
of the interior either. Herd 'em up, pack 'em off and give 'em
the inside room in the badlands. Let 'em be pinched, hurt,
hungry and dead up against it!. . . Personally, I hate
Japanese. And that goes for all of them.[14]

During this time, when irrational reasoning for the exclusion of all Japanese was to escalate, General DeWitt advanced a very specific point, that is, the Nisei, above all, should be excluded from the West Coast.

"In the war in which we are now engaged, racial affinities are not severed by migration. The Japanese race is an enemy race and while many second and third generation Japanese born on United States soil, possessed by United States citizenship, have become "Americanized," the racial strains are undiluted. To conclude otherwise is to expect that children born of white parents on Japanese soil lose all racial affinity and become loyal Japanese subjects, ready to fight and, if necessary, to die for Japan in a war against the nation of their parents. That Japan is allied with Germany and Italy in this struggle is no ground for assuming that any Japanese, barred from assimilation by convention as he is, though born and raised in the United States, will not turn against this nation when the final test of loyalty comes. It, therefore follows that along the vital Pacific Coast over 112,000 potential enemies of Japanese extraction are at large today."[15]

In the effort to encourage the wholesale removal of Japanese, Walter Lippmann wrote a racially biased editorial on his misdirected concern of the potential sabotage by the Japanese in the West Coast. Lippman, a prominent, respected columnist, on February 12, 1942, wrote to state that native-born Nisei as well as aliens are potential saboteurs, and should be removed from the West Coast. Lippmann argued, that due to the "eminent enemy attack on the United States", all persons should prove that he had a good reason to be there. Jumping on the bandwagon of Lippmann's suggestion of exclusion of Japanese from the West Coast, Westbrook Pegler wrote:

"Do you get what (Lippman) says? . . . The enemy has been scouting our coast. . . . The Japs ashore are communicating with the enemy offshore and . . . on the basis of · "what is known to be taking place" there are signs that a well-organized blow is being withheld only until it can do the most damage. . . . We are so dumb and considerate of the minute constitutional rights and even of the political feelings and influence of people whom we have every reason to anticipate with preventive action!"[16]

More FBI arrests were being made, and the implementation of the evacuation was formalized, ten weeks after the outbreak of the war on February 19, 1942, when President Roosevelt signed Executive Order 9066 which gave the Secretary of War and the military commanders authority and power to exclude any persons from the designated areas in order to provide fully secured national defense to guard against sabotage and espionage.

Many legislators criticized the loose language of the Order 9066. Senator Danaher wondered how a person would know what conduct constituted a violation of this act, an essential requirement for a criminal statue. Senator Taft spoke out against it. He stated:

"I think this is probably the "sloppiest" criminal law I have ever read or seen anywhere. I certainly think the Senate should not pass it. I do not want to object, because the purpose of it is understood. . . . (The bill) does not say who shall prescribe the restrictions. It does not say how anyone shall know that the restrictions are applicable to that particular zone. It does not appear that there is any authority given to anyone to prescribe any restriction. . . . I have no doubt an act of that kind would be enforced in war time. I have no doubt that in peacetime no man could ever be convicted under it, because the court would find that it was so indefinite and so uncertain that it could not be enforced under the Constitution."[17]

Implementation of the Executive Order
Thus, Secretary of War Stimson was empowered to implement Executive Order 9066. Under the power, General DeWitt, head of the Western Defense Command, was designated to execute this Order. The intent of Executive Order 9066 as written, directed all American citizens of Japanese descent, Japanese and German aliens and any persons suspected of being potentially dangerous were to be excluded from the designated military areas. Ultimately, everyone of Italian descent were omitted from any plan

70

of exclusion, noting that they were "potentially less dangerous as a whole."

Public Proclamation No. 1

By March 2, 1942, Public Proclamation No. 1 was issued, which announced as a matter of military necessity, the creation of Military areas 1 and 2. Military area 1 was the western half of Washington, Oregon and California and the southern half of Arizona and Military area 2 was designated as all portions of the states not included in Military area 1.

My father, after hearing and reading the threatening addresses, commentaries and remarks by public officials; issuance of Proclamation No. 1 and the creation of Military area 2 ("White Zone"); all these events convinced him that the only logical action was to "voluntarily" evacuate from San Jose.

Many such "voluntary" evacuations actually began before the issuance of Executive Order 9066, or the Public Proclamation No. 1. After the announcement of Public Proclamation No. 1, and by March 2, 1942, 2005 of the 107,500 Japanese and Japanese Americans living in Military area No. 1, moved out. Between March 12 to June 30, 1942, 10,312 persons of Japanese ancestry reported their "voluntary" intention to move out of Military area No. 1. Of the 10,312 registered, only 4,889 left the area as part of the "voluntary" program. Of these voluntary migrants, 1,963 went to Colorado, 1,519 to Utah, 305 to Idaho, 205 to eastern Washington, 115 to eastern Oregon, the remainder must be assumed to have relocated in the interior of California and to the other states.

Hearing that the Tanaka and the Koga families were making plans to relocate immediately to Central California, the bargain hunters, unethical public, and scavengers all invaded our farm and household. People came into our house, bargaining with my father on the furniture. Some offered $50 for the entire household of furniture, my father begged off the first few offers, yet finding that he could not get no more than the original offer, sold all our furniture including the kitchen and bedroom equipment, with the exception of the stove, refrigerator and beds, and other minimal necessities for needed for existence in Central California.

My father related later, that he had received $300 for the six acres of vegetables ready for harvest and $150 for the new tractor with its plow, cultivator, seeder and other miscellaneous equipment purchased a few years earlier. My father although beaten by these insensitive "white" farmers and bargain hunters, stated to the family: "The important thing is to keep the family together, money and wealth, we can again strive for, but our lives, we cannot replace." After a week of this informal "auction" my father disposed of all the items which he did not need in Dinuba. Father later stated: "We have recaptured 5 to 10 percent of the worth of our farm equipment and furniture, and approximately that same percentage for the crops. What a windfall for the white farmers. "It is unfair! It is unfair!"

Humiliation and a feeling of despair was felt by my father as he "gave away" our life earnings, the total worth of the Koga and Tanaka families. If it wasn't for his determination to keep his family out of the dreaded assembly and relocation camps, (being freely discussed during this era), or grandfather's possible re-arrest, he certainly would have stayed longer in San Jose, which would have given him more time to harvest the crops and possibly bargain for a higher value on all the properties that were disposed earlier in haste.

Due to the insensitivities of the buyers of Japanese properties (items such as autos, furniture, farm equipment, art objects, etc.), it was purported the evacuees angered by the indignations of the unscrupulous buyers of offering a fraction of the value for their properties, placed ads in local papers stating: "Evacuee desires to dispose of a new 1941 car." Fictitious address was noted in the ad. It was observed that the prospective buyers would ride around several times around the block trying to find the address; while the future evacuee chuckled and laughed as the parade of cars were not able to find the address.

By March 16, 1942, my father made all the arrangments to leave, saying their goodbyes and "sayonaras" the night before at a farewell party held at the community hall hosted by the "Trimble Road" area farmers. Father was singled out as a brave new pioneer who was going out to an unknown area to start a new life.

Many stated: "Shiga ta ga nai!" (It can't be helped!) We must do what is planned for us, whether it is an assembly center or a concentration camp. What else can we do? My father realizing that most of the "Trimble Road" farmers would not organize to fight the proposed forced relocation, or leave the area, just stated: "We need to leave and will join our friends in the interior of California."

The party again lasted into the early morning, causing our entire family to awake the next day at 8:00 a.m., two hours later than normal. After eating breakfast, a neighbor brought us enough "bento," to feed us for lunch and dinner. We gave our thanks for the "bento" and the farewell party, the night before, and we all pledged to meet again at the "Trimble Road" area after the duration of World War II.

Leaving was traumatic. We were the first to leave, forced by circumstances of war. Many of the families settling here since the early 1900's, now after 40 years had to leave. "Is this America? Is this justice?" There were now doubts raised on the validity of the constitutional rights protected by the United States Constitution. "Is one's home, his palace?"

We packed our suitcases, placed our household goods wrapped with newspaper in wooden crates and loaded the minimal furniture on my father's two-ton stake truck. Grandfather, grandmother and my two sisters moved into our new family car, a Buick, which was to be driven by my mother. My father purchased his car only one week prior to December 7, 1941. I was so proud to ride beside my father in the truck and again bid "goodbye" to neighbors as we started on our trek for the so-called "White Zone" in Central California.

On our arrival to Dinuba in the late afternoon of March 17, 1942, it was announced that the FBI having arrested 1,291 Japanese by December 10, 1941, had increased their arrest by February 16, 1942 to 2,198 Japanese. "What a relief!" My father stated. The entire family assured him that we made the right decision to relocate to Dinuba, and as we sat down and had dinner with the Haras', we all agreed that we were very grateful to be in Dinuba and that grandfather was not one of the 2,198 Japanese arrested and being sent to confinement for the duration of the war.

After the week of deciding various options left to us on whether to find or build a house, my father suggested to the family, that he could economically build a minimal house to be located on the Hara's property, by using the lumber and materials offered by them. After the war, the Haras' would also benefit by gaining an additional house on their property for their relatives or hired hands.

Proclamation No. 4

By March 29, 1942, Proclamation No. 4 was issued barring persons of Japanese ancestry from moving out of Military area No. 1, therefore, the systematic mandatory evacuation began. War Relocation Authority (WRA) selected and set up assembly centers throughout California, usually selected fairgrounds or racetracks for these centers with the exception of Pinedale and Sacramento in California, Portland, Oregon, and Mayer, Arizona.

Therefore, Japanese and Japanese-Americans were given seven-day notice to assemble in a specific location posted on telephone poles and other visual public posting spaces.

My father, hearing of Proclamation No. 4, expressed concern for our past neighbors—farmers at the "Trimble Road" area, for he knew by this Proclamation, they would be relocated into assembly centers. "How fortunate we are!" he stated.

Father again expressed thanks for the good fortune of knowing kind and caring persons such as the Haras', and set out the next day to construct "our house." My father, knowledgeable in carpentry, drew the foundation and floor plans; exterior elevations; and the section of the house indicating the framing members of the roof, floor and walls on "butcher paper." The next day, he started the construction. With the help of Mr. Hara's friend, this four bedroom house was constructed within two months, and was completed on May 19, 1942. The house now complete, we moved into "our house." We again expressed our gratefulness to the Haras, who gave up a portion of their house and also for giving father and the family the opportunity to build a house on their property.

Public Proclamation No 6

Public Proclamation No. 6, ordered by DeWitt, in early June, 1942, placed into motion the exclusion of Japanese aliens and American citizens from Military area 2 of California, which meant all of California would be evacuated on the grounds of "military necessity." My father became quite angry with this Proclamation, since earlier, "voluntary" evacuation of Japanese to the inland of California was encouraged and no suggestion was ever transmitted that this Military area 2 in California or any other state would be cleared of ethnic Japanese. "How can our government lie to us?" My father stated again: "Exclusion from California Military area 2, appears to have been decided without any additional evidence or threat of danger in this area, and I am angry because I sense that the decision to remove all Japanese from the West Coast must have been predetermined earlier."

Public Proclamation No. 7
On June 6, 1942, all Japanese had been evacuated from Military area No. 1 to assembly centers. General DeWitt, on June 8, 1942, issued Public Proclamation No. 7, which required all ethnic Japanese remaining in the area and not exempt, were ordered to report in person to the nearest assembly center. The forced mass exodus of Japanese and Japanese-Americans had begun.

Chapter 6
EXCLUSION, ASSEMBLY CENTERS
AND RELOCATION CAMPS

Exclusion

By 1942, there were approximately 120,000 Japanese in California, 50,000 Issei and 70,000 Nisei. The Nisei ranged from newly born to young adults. The largest percentage was in high school or college. Those who had graduated in the early 1940's prior to World War II from colleges or universities were having a difficult time securing work in their professions due to the orchestrated racial prejudice by many Californians.

Thus, by December 7, 1941, after the infamous bombing of Pearl Harbor by Japan, hysteria was easily raised, and all Japanese on the West Coast, whether citizens or not, were labeled as a "yellow peril." The public perception that the Japanese could not be trusted and must be excluded from their newly adopted home was recited over and over again, although California's historians can substantiate that many Japanese immigrants could claim that their families had arrived in 1868, or shortly thereafter, some seventy years before Pearl Harbor. No other immigrant group until this time, had ever been accused of disloyalty or required to prove their loyalty to the United States, because of race.

A total of 126,947 Japanese who resided in the continental United States, only 15,000 lived outside the western states. Therefore, only those few living outside of the western states did not lose their constitutional rights of due process under the law.

The lengthy predetermined conclusion was very clear: Many Californians saw that the war to be an opportunity to exclude the Japanese who were becoming fierce competitors in agriculture, horticulture, fishing and commerce, unfairly became being perceived as a threat to their economic gains. Others schooled for seven decades on the threat of the "yellow peril" accepted and encouraged the relocation of 120,000 Japanese, most of them citizens of the United States.

The agriculturalists and small business ventures who promoted and succeeded in the wholesale removal of Japanese farmers and businessmen prospered during the war years. Many racist agriculturalists as well as others during this time acquired land once occupied or leased by the Japanese. They accumulated large parcels of farm land which eventually translated in later years to a value of millions of dollars of real estate. Therefore, agriculturalists in their efforts and support to exclude their competition gained great rewards for this deliberate elimination of Japanese from farming and other ventures.

The final result was the approved incarceration of citizens of America without counsel or due process of law.

America's Concentration Camps
"It is sobering to recall that though the Japanese relocation program, carried through at such incalculable cost in misery and tragedy, was justified to us on the grounds that the Japanese were potentially disloyal, yet the record does not disclose a single case of Japanese disloyalty or sabotage during the whole war. . .

It is easier to say what loyalty is not than to say what it is. It is not conformity. It is not passive acquiescence in the status quo. It is not preference for everything American over everything foreign. It is not an ostrich-like ignorance of other countries and other institutions. It is not the indulgence in ceremony—a flag salute, an oath of allegiance, a fervid verbal declaration. It is not a particular creed, a particular version of history, a particular body of economic practices, a particular philosophy. It is a tradition, an ideal, and a principle. It is a willingness to subordinate every private advantage for the larger good. It is an appreciation of the rich diverse contributions that can come from the most varied sources. It is allegiance to the traditions that have guided our greatest statesmen and inspired our most eloquent poets—the traditions of freedom, equality, democracy, tolerance, the traditions of the higher law, of experimentation, co-operation, and pluralism. It is a realization that America was born of revolt, flourished on dissent, became great through experimentation."[18]

Assembly Centers

On March 31, 1942, evacuation began and it took until August 7, 1942, to assemble all persons of Japanese ancestry into various assembly centers in Oregon, California and Arizona. It was estimated that about 92,000 persons were evacuated to the centers prior to being relocated into more permanent relocation camps. The following table identifies the assembly centers, population and dates of occupation:

TABLE 4[19]
ASSEMBLY CENTERS 1942

Assembly Centers	Maximum Population Number	Date to 1942		Dates Occupied From 1942		To 1942	
Puyallup	7,390	July	25	April	28	Sept.	12
Portland	3,676	June	6	May	2	Sept.	10
Maryville	2,451	June	2	May	8	June	29
Sacramento	4,739	May	30	May	6	June	26
Tanforan	7,816	July	25	April	28	Oct.	13
Stockton	4,271	May	21	May	10	Oct.	17
Turlock	3,661	June	2	April	30	Aug.	12
Salinas	3,586	June	23	April	27	July	4
Merced	4,508	June	3	May	6	Sept.	15
Pinedale	4,792	June	29	May	7	July	23
Fresno	5,120	Sept.	4	May	6	Oct.	30
Tulare	4,978	Aug.	11	April	20	Sept.	4
Santa Anita	18,719	July	20	March	27	Oct.	27
Pomona	5,434	July	20	May	7	Aug.	24
Mayer	245	May	25	May	7	June	4
Manzanar	9,837			March	21	June	2

1. Transferred to WRA for use as a relocation camp.

78

The Relocation Camp

While the first evacuees began arriving at relocation centers at the end of May 1942, my father in Dinuba was doing odd jobs prior to his decision to find a semi-permanent job till the duration of the war. He would learn later that General DeWitt will issue Public Proclamation No. 6 in early June, 1942, ordering all ethnic Japanese be cleared from California.

During this time, evacuees were being transferred from temporary assembly centers to relocation camps. By June 30, 1942, over 46,000 persons of Japanese descent were living in Manzanar, Poston and Tule Lake, three of ten permanent relocation camps. Reflecting bitterness of being lied to by the government, my father was enraged in reading the contents of DeWitt's Public Proclamation No. 6., stated: Again, the politicians and the agricultural interests are pushing for the expansion of the exclusison zone for their economic gains. By early June, the exclusionists were successful in convincing the military that the removal of all Japanese would guarantee "complete security and remove the threat and danger in this area." The Final Report lamely explains this change:

Military area No. 2, in California must be evacuated because:

1. Geographically and strategically the eastern boundry of the State of California approximates the easternly limit of Military Area No. 1 in Washington and Orgeon . . . and because
2. The natural forests and mountain barriers from which it was determined to exclude all Japanese, lie in Military area no. 2 in California, although these lie in Military Area No. 1 of Washington and Oregon.

This analysis for the decision of removal of Japanese from Area No. 2 is absurd. Eastern boundry of California lies more than 100 miles east of the Military Area No. 1 at the Oregon border.

Public Proclamation No. 6

After the issuance of Public Proclamation No. 6, all Japanese in Central California were mobilized to be removed. Again, my father had to inventory all the items he bought from San Jose. His new Buick he had purchased one month previous to December

79

7, 1941 for $800, was sold for $200 dollars. His truck was sold for $300, only a fraction of the total cost. The remaining furniture and kitchen stove, refrigerator and a room heater were sold for less than $100.

Clothing, a small Buddhist shrine (obutsudan), hidden throughout the many months of exodus, were the only items that were left after 40 years of struggle in the United States. Questions of the unfair struggle the Japanese had to endure and the unconstitutional proposed incarceration were raised by my father and others, again and again, yet, the few champions of civil rights had no influence on the public's orchestrated edict to remove the Japanese from their homes. My father had commented: "How unfair how unfair. I have served my country, (reflecting his tour in the U.S. Navy at his early age), yet, I get kicked on and am becoming destroyed. Is this America?"

After the housekeeping was completed, windows and doors plywooded down and secure, all items sold or given away, the Haras and the our family followed instructions of the public notices posted on telephone poles, or other public area, announcing that all Japanese must report to a certain designated area on a given time and date for their journey to the relocation camps. Prior to being sent to the relocation camp, all evacuees were required to get identification tags for their family and luggage.

I have read many articles of families having to go after these tags at police stations or other designated public offices, and as I could reflect, I have asked my mother if she could recall the incident when we as a family had to get these tags and wear them for the identification of ourselves and our luggage.

Mother, paused, tears in her eyes, reflected for a moment, then stated:

"Son, your father and I, as I can recall, went to the police headquarters to register the family. We had a total of five members in our immediate family, and including your grandfather and grandmother, our total extended family was seven. As you might recall, the range in age of you children was from ten to seven months old. Your father and I came back from the police station with tags, I believe being consecutively numbered in the 70,000 series. Each number was in pairs, one was to be placed on your clothing, visable throughout our journey to the concentration camps and the second identical number was for the one piece of luggage you were allowed to take."

"I remember placing tags on you children, and the adults placed it on themselves, and father got all seven additional tags and affixed it to the boxes and luggages that housed our clothing. This act of placing and soon becoming only numbers, instead of free individuals, reminded me of that time, that we must be criminals who committed a crime, for only people incarcerated would be required to wear these identifications. How else could I have reacted! I lost my traditional freedom, my dignity and soon will be incarcerated behind barbed wires! How could this happen to me? I committed no crime! Who protects the innocent? Is this democracy? Will this nightmare ever end?"

After the identificaiton process was completed, the luggage was thrown into the awaiting box cars and the evacuees were herded like cattle into coaches with shades drawn (to hide the Japanese traveling throughout California). The trains were powered by several engines pulling a long length of cars as it headed toward Poston Camp 3 Relocation Camp.

By late September, 1942, all the centers except Jerome had been opened and 90,000 people had been incarcerated. Then by November 1, 1942, relocation of all Japanese from the West Coast and Arizona had been completed and at the end of the war, centers' population increased to an all time high of 106,770 people. The following Table 5 indicates that 120,315 persons of Japanese decent were held in custody of WRA.

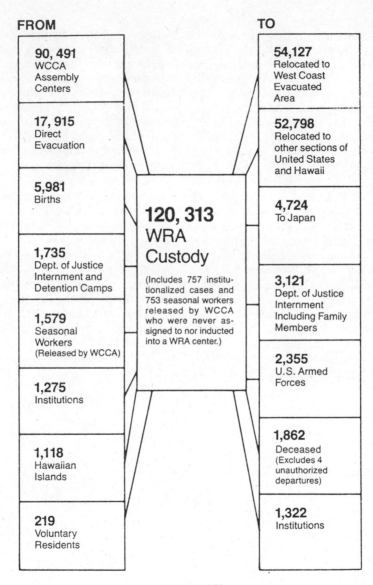

FROM

90, 491
WCCA
Assembly
Centers

17, 915
Direct
Evacuation

5,981
Births

1,735
Dept. of Justice
Internment and
Detention Camps

1,579
Seasonal
Workers
(Released by WCCA)

1,275
Institutions

1,118
Hawaiian
Islands

219
Voluntary
Residents

120, 313
WRA
Custody

(Includes 757 institutionalized cases and 753 seasonal workers released by WCCA who were never assigned to nor inducted into a WRA center.)

TO

54,127
Relocated to
West Coast
Evacuated
Area

52,798
Relocated to
other sections of
United States
and Hawaii

4,724
To Japan

3,121
Dept. of Justice
Internment
Including Family
Members

2,355
U.S. Armed
Forces

1,862
Deceased
(Excludes 4
unauthorized
departures)

1,322
Institutions

TABLE 5[20]
TOTAL JAPANESE EVACUEES

PLATE 4

WESTERN DEFENSE COMMAND AND FOURTH ARMY
WARTIME CIVIL CONTROL ADMINISTRATION
Presidio of San Francisco, California
May 3, 1942

INSTRUCTIONS
TO ALL PERSONS OF
JAPANESE
ANCESTRY
Living in the Following Area:

All of that portion of the County of Alameda, State of California, within the boundary beginning at the point where the southerly limits of the City of Oakland meet San Francisco Bay; thence easterly and following the southerly limits of said city to U. S. Highway No. 50; thence southerly and easterly on said Highway No. 50 to its intersection with California State Highway No. 21; thence southerly on said Highway No. 21 to its intersection, at or near Warm Springs, with California State Highway No. 17; thence southerly on said Highway No. 17 to the Alameda-Santa Clara County line; thence westerly and following said county line to San Francisco Bay; thence northerly, and following the shoreline of San Francisco Bay to the point of beginning.

Pursuant to the provisions of Civilian Exclusion Order No. 34, this Headquarters, dated May 3, 1942, all persons of Japanese ancestry, both alien and non-alien, will be evacuated from the above area by 12 o'clock noon, P. W. T., Saturday, May 9, 1942.

No Japanese person living in the above area will be permitted to change residence after 12 o'clock noon, P. W. T., Sunday, May 3, 1942, without obtaining special permission from the representative of the Commanding General, Northern California Sector, at the Civil Control Station located at:

920 - "C" Street,
Hayward, California.

Such permits will only be granted for the purpose of uniting members of a family, or in cases of grave emergency.

The Civil Control Station is equipped to assist the Japanese population affected by this evacuation in the following ways:

1. Give advice and instructions on the evacuation.

2. Provide services with respect to the management, leasing, sale, storage or other disposition of most kinds of property, such as real estate, business and professional equipment, household goods, boats, automobiles and livestock.

3. Provide temporary residence elsewhere for all Japanese in family groups.

4. Transport persons and a limited amount of clothing and equipment to their new residence.

The Following Instructions Must Be Observed:

1. A responsible member of each family, preferably the head of the family, or the person in whose name most of the property is held, and each individual living alone, will report to the Civil Control Station to receive further instructions. This must be done between 8:00 A. M. and 5:00 P. M. on Monday, May 4, 1942, or between 8:00 A. M. and 5:00 P. M. on Tuesday, May 5, 1942.

2. Evacuees must carry with them on departure for the Assembly Center, the following property:

(a) Bedding and linens (no mattress) for each member of the family;
(b) Toilet articles for each member of the family;
(c) Extra clothing for each member of the family;
(d) Sufficient knives, forks, spoons, plates, bowls and cups for each member of the family;
(e) Essential personal effects for each member of the family.

All items carried will be securely packaged, tied and plainly marked with the name of the owner and numbered in accordance with instructions obtained at the Civil Control Station. The size and number of packages is limited to that which can be carried by the individual or family group.

3. No pets of any kind will be permitted.

4. No personal items and no household goods will be shipped to the Assembly Center.

5. The United States Government through its agencies will provide for the storage, at the sole risk of the owner, of the more substantial household items, such as iceboxes, washing machines, pianos and other heavy furniture. Cooking utensils and other small items will be accepted for storage if crated, packed and plainly marked with the name and address of the owner. Only one name and address will be used by a given family.

6. Each family, and individual living alone, will be furnished transportation to the Assembly Center or will be authorized to travel by private automobile in a supervised group. All instructions pertaining to the movement will be obtained at the Civil Control Station.

**Go to the Civil Control Station between the hours of 8:00 A. M. and 5:00 P. M.,
Monday, May 4, 1942, or between the hours of 8:00 A. M. and 5:00 P. M.,
Tuesday, May 5, 1942, to receive further instructions.**

J. L. DeWITT
Lieutenant General, U. S. Army
Commanding

SEE CIVILIAN EXCLUSION ORDER NO. 34.

Instructions to all persons of Japanese ancestry.

The following Table 6 indicates the capacity of various relocation camps:

TABLE 6[21]
RELOCATION CAMPS

Name		Location		Capacity (in persons)
Central Utah	(Topaz)	West-Central	Utah	10,000
Colorado River	(Poston)			
Unit 1		Western	Arizona	10,000
Unit 2		Western	Arizona	5,000
Unit 3		Western	Arizona	5,000
Gila River	(Rivers)			
Butte Camp		Central	Arizona	10,000
Canal Camp		Central	Arizona	5,000
Granada	(Amache)	Southeastern	Colorado	8,000
Heart Mountain		Northwestern	Wyoming	12,000
Jerome	(Denson)	Southeastern	Arkansas	10,000
Manzanar		East-Central	California	10,000
Minidoka	(Hunt)	South-Central	Idaho	10,000
Rohwer		Southeastern	Arkansas	10,000
Tule Lake	(Newell)	North-Central	California	10,000

After arriving in Parkerville, Arizona, heckled and jeered by the unfriendly citizenry, the internees were herded into buses on to their journey to Relocation Camp: Poston Camp 3. Upon arrival to this camp, quarters were assigned, and all families headed toward their barrack confines. Barracks were constructed of minimum standards with loose, knotty boards over a single layer of tar paper and open wood stud interiors. During construction, some of the tar paper would be torn, and knots dropped out of some of the boards as the wet boards dried; daylight, dust, wind and privacy became a problem. Therefore, harsh winter nights and hot summer desert temperatures became part of the interior environment of the barracks. Cross partitions separating another family were no better constructed, thus ingenious families placed home-made draperies which served as a privacy screen as well as a limited sound barrier screen between each family quarters.

Old and the young became the first victims of the desert camps. Heat in the 120 degree temperature was common, and many who were residing a few days before, in moderate temperatures in coastal areas became a part of the statistics. Therefore, a makeshift cemetery had to be initiated.

Food was initially a problem. Food supplies originally were being diverted for civilian use by the soldiers and military personnel, yet, as the Japanese residents became more organized and started to govern themselves within the camps, supplies and materials were stringently checked to insure that confiscation by the military personnel of the camp did not occur any longer. Eventually, the Japanese internees manned and organized the supplies. Thus, policing and control of materials and supplies became less necessary, since it was understood morally and culturally, that stealing from other Japanese is like "stealing from one's self."

Hygiene, although not convenient, was less a problem. Female internees needed to get used to open gang showers, and latrines and bath houses were located in the center of the block, some one-eighth mile distance from some residents. The old and the young suffered through these conditions. Some had to be carried to these facilities due to their physically handicapped conditions. The entire camp life became for many, a great struggle and a individual challenge for survival.

Many hardships existed in the camps, yet Isseis were afforded a well-deserved time off. They had worked without rest and relaxation for their 40 years of selfless drudgery. Evacuees, the Isseis, after some time in camp, adjusted to the environment and their artistic and horticultural expressions were translated in their personal gardens and entries. Landscaped mounds, fish ponds, bonsai trees, and other "Japanese" cultural experiences were now being transformed onto the harsh desert scene.

Although living in camp became seemingly normal, all were reminded that they were prisoners, confined behind barbed wires, guarded by rifled military guards. Those who tried to escape were either shot or at best apprehended and warned. This reminder was constantly advanced by the military personnel to insure against break outs.

Schools were established from grades kindergarten to the twelfth grades and a serious attempt was made to meet the standards of Arizona. Due to the varied training and maturity of the teachers, different classes were adequate at times, while, others had certain short comings. During the period of 1942–1945, educational deficiencies for some of the students in the camps may had had certain effects on their success in higher education; yet, as a whole, this generation of Americans became the most highly educated segment of an ethnic or majority group in America.

442 Combat Team, "Go for Broke"

While still incarcerated in relocation camps behind barbed wires guarded by gun-pointing sentries, the young Niseis having, the love for their country, and the unwritten agenda that they were loyal Americans, volunteered in the Army from all of the so called "relocation camps" in the United States. Some Japanese incarcerated in "camps," questioned the rationale for this determined decision of volunteering in the Army. Many of the incarcerated stated: "You have been incarcerated as enemy agents; a menace to the public; disloyal, untrustworthy citizens of the United States, stripped of your constitutional rights under 'due process;' and with those accusations; you are volunteering to defend the country that failed you. 'Why? Why?' " The volunteers stated: "Because we know we are loyal Americans. America needs us, so we must defend America."

It will be recorded later by contemporary sociologists that the one important underlying reason for the mass volunteering into the armed forces was that they now had an opportunity, once and for all, to announce to America, in no uncertain terms, that Japanese-Americans were Americans first, loyal, trustworthy and could be counted on when the need arose.

The "Go for Broke" 442nd Combat Team, attached to the 100th Battalion, valiantly fought in Italy against overwhelming odds, and due to the heavy losses suffered by the 100th Battalion, it became known as the "Purple Heart Battalion." The 422nd Combat Team absorbing the 100th as its 1st Battalion went on to fight in France and Germany. . . . The 422nd went on to save the Texas' "Lost Battalion," . . . Great valor of the 422nd Nisei Combat Team earned them the honor of the United States Army's most decorated unit. Laudatory statements also enhanced the "Go for Broke" image: "The courage, steadfastness and willingness of your officers and men were equal to any ever displayed by United States troops, reads a message to the 442nd from the Texas 36th Division.[22]

"I have followed closely your splendid record . . . I have seen you in action and know your ability," General Mark Clark said in a statement to the 100th Battalion.

A message from the 168th Infantry read:

"In appreciation of the heroic and meritorious achievement of our fellow Americans in the 100th Battalion and 442nd Infantry Regiment, we do hereby assert that you are fully deserving of all the privileges with which we are ourselves bestowed."[23]

All the nation lauded the valiant display of courage and love for country displayed by the so called previous "untrustworthy, disloyal" Nisei soldiers of the 422nd Combat Team, and a hero's welcome tickertape parade followed, as they returned from Europe. No American could say, henceforth, that Japanese-Americans were less than the patriotic loyal Americans we all are!

Chapter 7
ON THE JOURNEY HOME

Return

Prior to the return of Japanese-Americans to the West Coast, boards of supervisors, city councils, and even the California state legislature were debating whether they should allow the Japanese and Japanese-Americans to return to California.

Although most boards of supervisors or city councils of various counties and cities of California did not discuss any matters regarding Japanese during their exclusion, it was noted in 1943, that the Santa Clara County Board of Supervisors unanimously voted to send a telegram to the federal government to protest the release of Japanese from the relocation camps and their subsequent return to California. The San Jose City Council voted a split five to two to continue the exclusion of Japanese from San Jose.

Even a Gold Star mother, Mrs. Benaphal, who would later learn of the valor of the 442nd Nisei Regiment, told the California State Senate Committee on her opinion on whether Japanese should be allowed to return to the West Coast stated:

> We want to keep the Japs out of California.
> State Senator Slater: For the duration?
> Mrs. Benaphal: No for all times.
> State Senator Slater: That's the stuff!"[24]

After the war ended in 1945, Japanese packed their meager belongings to return to their original or newly selected homes. Relocation camps soon would vanish in the frigid cold or hot desert environment forever. The federal government under the War Relocation Authority (WRA) was authorized to give travel fare and a minimal cash payments to all residents of camps similar to prisoners' benefits given prior to their release from prison.

My father, who was adventurous and contemporary of mind, suggested to the family that, this would be a great opportunity to see and feel the vibrancy of the different parts of America. Father suggested that we should venture to New York, since it was not only the furthermost part of the United States from California, but played an important part in American history. Thus, he announced that he was offered a job at a winery in New York. Mother stated: "Winery? Do you know anything about making wines?" Father assured mother that he was a good agriculturalist and grape growing could not be that difficult, and further stated: "I like wine, I drink wine, and I know my wines." Grandfather's opinion and decision was solicited by mother and father and grandfather stated: "Anata nei makashi toku." ("I will leave it up to you to make the decision").

My proud grandfather who struggled for forty years in the United States prior to the war, the hardworking farmer, never burdensome to his family or society was now feeling the trauma for his life and survival in his adopted land, America. How can it be that one who has been a good citizen, good neighbor, a good provider, by this exclusion, now is less a man than his counterparts in America. "What happened to the cherished principles that America was built on, individual freedom for all ? How can it be that a country with such high ideals of democracy and independence, would turn on me? Now, after more than forty years of struggle, and now being more than 60 years of age, I am tired and will have to relinquish my reign as Patriarch to my son-in-law, my father, by making the statement: 'Ana ta nei maka shi toku.' (I will leave all arrangements to you.)"

Father made all necessary preparations with the War Relocation Authority (WRA), to leave as soon as possible, by completing and processing the required papers and received clearance to leave. He made arrangements to leave the following day. We bid farewell to all our friends the night before at a small going away party held in the mess hall and hosted by our friends. We got to sleep by midnight, yet no one in the family could sleep soundly, since all of us were experiencing great anxieties of having to travel to the furthermost strange eastern state in the United States, New York. Most of our friends, who were making plans to return to California, their home state, kidded grandfather and grandmother by stating: "Why are you letting your son-in-law dictate your fate by taking you to such a foreign area?" "You will again find racial prejudice all over again." "Come with us, we will house you, New York, a foreign state, is no place for an Issei." (Japanese returning to California after World War II will find great racial tension and prejudice awaiting them, while on the eastern coast racial prejudice was minimal or non-existent.)

I was very proud of grandfather that night when he stated: "There are those of you who will never explore beyond your backyard. How shallow! There are wondrous, different and exciting adventures awaiting all of you if you look beyond your backyards. We are going to explore America, but please leave a space in your heart for me in the future for we shall return after this adventure." My father and mother hugged grandfather, grandmother had tears in her eyes, and we children learned what a strong and wise immigrant my grandfather was.

The next day, we left by bus to Parkerville, Arizona, boarded a train and headed east. Within three days, we reached Fredonia, New York, and we latter will learn that Fredonia was close to Niagra Falls. After about a year and half in New York, my father discussed a planned time table for our return to California. My father suggested on our return to the West Coast, would be to travel to Detroit, Michigan where family friends, the Reverend Sakow, Buddhist minister and his family resided. Father worked in Detroit at a carpet cleaning and dying company, and I reflect the side benefits due to this employment were that our entire abode was carpeted by remnants he would sew together in his off hours to create room area rugs.

Father worked in Detroit at the carpet cleaning and dying company for four years, and shortly after that, started farming (his great love), in Davison, Michigan. At Davison, he pioneered raising lettuce, by experimenting with the season, temperature and hybrid lettuce seeds. Within a few years, he would become the "Lettuce King" in Michigan. His pioneering and experimentation would eventually lead to the successful growing of lettuce, and singlehandedly, created a major agricultural crop, which expanded the entire agricultural industry in Michigan. Farmers from all parts of Michigan and the surrounding states emerged on to my father's farm to learn of the techniques and seasonal growing cycles of lettuce. Today, there are a large expanse of lettuce fields cultivated due to my father's experimentation. It was reported that by this expanded growth of the lettuce crop in Michgian, effects were being felt in many parts of California.

After six years of farming in Michigan, father returned to California with his family, and established a landscape gardening business and operated a produce stand prior to his retirement. Although many families moved to the east and midwest after the War, a large portion of them returned to California. (However, it can be substantiated that the majority of the Japanese families, both Issei and Nisei returned directly to California and the West Coast after World War II from the various relocation camps throughout the United States.)

The Issei and Nisei parents who returned directly to California immediately after the war were served notice by many white inhabitants that they were not wanted in their towns and neighborhoods. These acts were very confusing to the new returnees. Had we not been obedient, right or wrong, and paid our dues by the incarceration placed upon us? Hadn't we shown our bravery by the sacrifices made by our sons? Why are we being treated like this? Do the Issei parents who had sacrificed their offspring earlier during World War II, as members of the 442nd "Go for Broke" Combat Team, (the most decorated regiment in U.S. history) again need to prove that Japanese were loyal and trustworthy Americans. This caused great anger to the thousands of returnees. Do we have to once again disapprove the popular myth and fabrication of the following: The Issei came to California, with one thing in mind! . . . make money and return to Japan . . . yet his gaining of wealth or return to Japan never materialized."

The Issei found again he was confronted with isolated incidents of prejudice and racial tension, which created a deterrent in pursuing his enterprises. He will soon find solace in the fact that he wouldn't be alone in this fight since he would soon relinquish the patriarch to his son or son-in-law. It will soon be the fight of his offspring.

The Nisei

Prior to the 1940's, the Nisei only occasionally associated with the majority "white" population. Yet, after World War II and their subsequent return to California, the Niseis made an all out effort to start associating with his/her neighbors, contrary to the behavioral pattern of the Issei, since the greater society began to accept them. Although they felt racial tensions since occasional derogatory remarks were being issued by some, the Niseis quietly went on with their various enterprises or other professional and business ventures. The high school age Niseis or Sanseis at this time became the generation that were directed by the Issei or older Nisei parents to pursue education for the advancement of not only the individual, but more importantly to show America that Japanese are in fact, good or better citizens than any other Americans. This became their challenge.

The Sansei

The third generation Japanese-Americans having Nisei parents are Sansei. What are the goals of the Sansei? What are their expectations? The Sansei, today, have been completely assimilated in the mainstream of the American society, contrary to their forefathers and parents prior to 1941, who by design isolated themselves. They now have the same problems, concerns and involvements most Americans of this age will have, while many are searching for their cultural identity.

The removal of cultural identity was a deliberate program initiated by their Sansei parents. Having experienced hate and distrust not only due to their former isolationist behavior, but being constantly harrassed and accused of not being loyal or trustworthy to America, for being "Japanese", the Nisei parents, began a very calculated program to eliminate anything "Japanese." This process of removal or de-emphasis of the Japanese culture was a program that was pre-determined, creating great pains for the aesthetic and cultured Issei and older Nisei.

Resettlement

After the return of the Japanese to California, at the end of the war, Japanese families were again required to be communal for their own protection and security. Only Buddhist temples or other organizations friendly to Japanese having large halls became havens for the fortnight and sometimes months till the families found their own abodes.

In the process of finding other places to reside after the ordeal of the relocation camps, "urban Japanese familes," in Los Angeles and San Francisco tended to concentrate in certain core areas of the city which became to be known as "Japantown" or Nihonmachi. These unique areas have been in most part destroyed or removed due to the redevelopment processes initiated by the cities. Therefore, again, the displacement of many Japanese from the core area of the cities to other parts took place, creating permanent isolation for many.

Contrary to urban dwellers, the "suburban Japanese families," whether deliberate or not, scattered into various neighborhoods never trying to ghettorize themselves. One could only observe that this process may be a direct reaction of the racial tension caused by the isolation from the greater community and communal concentration of Japanese families prior to World War II.

A few years after resettlement into generally white neighborhoods, Japanese kept up their homes and grounds in immaculate conditions occasionally socialized with their neighbors. Their initial behavioral trait was of being semi-isolationist, because they were not sure at first whether they would be accepted by their white counterparts. Thus, their original behavioral pattern was a daily courteous "hello," and later as the comfort factor heightened with more frequent contacts, normal social behaviors such as one joining in for a coffee, a drink or an occasional dinner started to be realized.

Other experiences by Japanese families moving into white neighborhoods were not pleasant. Petitions were circulated at times, noting that a certain Japanese family was not welcomed. Prior to a Japanese buying a home in a particular neighborhood, the real estate company handling the transaction was told that they do not want "Jap" families in their neighborhood, therefore were instructed not to sell to Japanese. Others were more blatant in their acts to keeping Japanese completely out of their neighborhood. In working with a friendly real estate company handling the sale of the house, a "written, unofficial sales offer" was always in the files of the realtor, to show to prospective Japanese buyers, which resulted in the total exclusion of Japanese in that particular neighborhood.

Generally, Japanese children, growing up in California, during 1945—1950's, were somewhat treated differently than most other children. There were incidents reported where racial slurs were advanced, and rocks being thrown because the boy or girl was "Jap", and symbolized their former enemy. Thus, again Japanese families were required to congregate with other Japanese families for the purpose of protection. Although various isolated racial violences were reported by Japanese-American families during this era, the climate began to normalize, and Japanese-Americans became more generally accepted by their neighbors and their co-workers.

Prior to becoming "acceptable Americans," the Japanese parents began their program for the total "Americanization" of their children. Due to this societal change in attitude and their removal of anything "Japanese," the Japanese-Americans no longer needed the communal existence with their fellow Japanese for protection or accommodations, and finally being accepted as "real Americans," the Japanese parent began to feel for the first time, although limited at first, a real part of the American fabric.

First in the process of "total Americanization," was to create a plan to de-emphasize anything related to Japanese culture. Therefore, some, desiring to be more fully assimulated in the American society, and wanting of becoming totally accepted, even went so far as making drastic moral and ethical changes such as converting to Christianity from Buddhism. Others trying to enhance further acceptance by the majority of the American society, started to pronounce their ethnic names to sound Anglo, or European. Ohara started to sound Irish, yet names like Mineta became to be mistaken to be a name of an Italian family.

The second process which the parents considered key for the acceptance of the race was education. They asked themselves: "Who could deny us if we became leaders and front runners in our profession?" What we need to do is to educate all our children so that they need not farm, work in the fields like we parents, but be in business or a profession where pride and respect will be the child's reward. The Sanseis' parents stated: "We no longer can and will perpetuate the stereotype that Japanese are farmers and gardeners, for one can be anything one desires! Farming is at best, a gamble, a marginal business and we want our children to have a better life than toil with the soil, fight the weather, and worry about other environmental constraints to make a living.

We want our children to have a better life than us, free from prejudices, racial biases and the way we do this is to educate our children to be the best. If you are the best, who could criticize you, who could deny you? Yes, this is our goal, to educate our children, to give them a good life, and above all, once and for all, Japanese, for the first time, be accepted in the total American social structure. Yes, this is our mandate, this is our goal, we shall do it!" These are isolated conscensus opinions and comments of the Issei and Nisei parents of high school and college age children during the beginning of the 1950 era.

Therefore, with this emphasis of creating a complete success oriented generation, the Issei and Nisei parents' goals were to direct their offspring to become exceptional social and economic assets for America. "If our children are well-educated, better educated than any generation in America, history will recite the contributions of the Japanese-Americans, and they will become visible as an economic and social force in America. This challenge was fulfilled, since these Nisei and Sansei offspring became the most educated minority and or majority in U.S. history. It is purported that approximately 80 to 85 percent of Japanese-Americans during this era between 1945-1960's have acquired business, college or university level education.

The young Nisei and Sansei are a unique American product who have little cultural interface. The results are very clear. Within one generation the Sanseis now speak perfect English, without any ethnic accent, are perfectly comfortable and accepted in the majority white society, highly educated, and leaders in their community, profession and workplace. The end result was that the Nisei and Sansei became a public relations vehicle to say to America: Japanese are good citizens, they can achieve and are an asset to society. This particular experience relative to this generation has been successful. For how long, time will tell.

The Nisei and Sansei in the 1950's worried about the grades, dated, enjoyed the movies, visited drive-in restaurants, and in general enjoyed the association with other Japanese their age. They watched TV, studied intensely and were generally given the distinction in school to be the most studious and intelligent, yet on the whole, the child's motivation supported by the constant support by one's parents, contributed to his/her success in school. One only wonders if the following generations of Sansei and Yonsei will be as highly motivated as their predecessors?

Chapter 8
LEGAL ISSUES

Review of Cases
Honorable Judge Wayne Kanemoto

The legal issues raised by the drastic government actions all came in four separate cases, before the United States Supreme Court, for review.

Korematsu, Hirabayashi and Yasui Cases
The first three cases, Korematsu, Hirabayashi and Yasui, involved the issues of exclusion and evacuation along with that of curfew applied to American citizens of Japanese ancestry the Supreme Court ruled that the Wars Powers of the government permitted these drastic actions during wartime emergency.

These cases and their rulings, however, were quite anomalous in that the Government had never proved and the courts never required proof of any actual threat nor acts of sabotage, espionage or subversive acts on the part of Americans of Japanese ancestry. Only the hypothetical and the possible threat was discussed, and there never was shown, as traditionally required, that there was indeed, "a clear and present danger."

And, further, the U.S. Supreme Court never came to grips with nor discussed the subject of denial or due process in a setting where civil government was functioning within the area in question and where no such emergency existed that called for martial law as there was in Hawaii.

In the Korematsu case, which involved the issue of exclusion and evacuation, Justice Robert H. Jackson dissented stating: "The Principle lies about like a loaded weapon ready for the hand of any authority that can bring forward a plausible claim of an urgent need."

Justice Frank Murphy also dissented in that case and stated that the evacuation was "one of the most sweeping and complete deprivation of constitutional rights in the history of this nation in absence of martial law."

Endo Case

The fourth case to come before the U.S. Supreme Court, the Endo case, involved the denial of a writ of habeas corpus, a demand for release on the grounds that no charges been filed against the evacuee-internee.

In reviewing this case, the U.S. Supreme Court, while finding it unnecessary to reach and discuss the subject of denial of due process, found the detention to be unlawful in that Congress had authorized no prolonged detention in any of its enabling acts, and, accordingly, ordered the internee (and anyone else in similar circumstances) to be released forthwith. This decision, however, came down in the closing days of 1944, when most evacuees had been excluded and detained for more than two and one-half years.

These decisions have been part of legal history now for more than 40 years, but the recent Korematsu case was reopened in 1983. Korematsu petitioned the Federal District in San Francisco for dismissal of his 1942 conviction on the rare and unusual grounds of newly discovered evidence which showed deliberate distortion, falsification and concealment of facts which were given as ground for the emergency and the "military necessity" for the insurance of Executive Order 9066. The U.S. Department of Justice declined to contest the petition by defending the Government's 1942 position (presumably because it was indefensible). The record of Korematsu's conviction was set aside and dismissed. He is now petitioning the U.S. Supreme Court to set aside its ruling.

It also appears that similar dismissals will be forthcoming in the other two cases: the Hirabayashi and Yasui cases.

The Japanese Americans and the Courts
Steven T. Wing

One of the most astounding things that occurred during the evacuation and incarceration of the 120,000 Japanese-Americans during World War II was the lack of any significant protest acted largely in response to political and economic pressure fueled by wartime hysteria and prejudice.

Our most important Constitutional guarantees give people the right to property, to earn a living, and most importantly, to liberty and freedom. These rights can only be taken away when the government brings justifiable charges. In 1942, the federal government denied these constitutional rights to the Japanese-Americans. The federal courts, designed to uphold the Constitution and ensure that every individual is guaranteed his/her rights, failed miserably and forty years later have not reversed. itself and declared their earlier decisions to be wrong.

Part of history of Japanese-Americans is the larger fight against Executive Order 9066. Any one of the 120,000, who were forcibly removed, could have challenged the evacuation and internment orders in court, and each would have received the same decision given Fred Korematsu, Minoru Yasui and Gordon Hirabayshi by the United States Supreme Court. The Supreme Court's decisions in their cases upheld the justification presented by the government and, despite being three of the most widely cited, debated and denounced legal decisions, still stand as the law of the land.

The Landmark Wartime Cases
Minoru Yasui was convicted in 1942 for violating military curfew orders aimed at Japanese-Americans. He violated the curfew order purposely because he thought it was wrong. In addition to his later internment, Yasui spent nine months in solitary confinement in county jail.

Gordon Hirabayashi, convicted both for violating the curfew order and for refusing to report to a civil control station in 1942, served a total of two years in county jails and federal prisons. Hirabayashi has said that the only charge against him was his ancestry. If he had been charged with espionage or some crime, he would have been able to defend himself.

Fred Korematsu, similarly convicted in 1942 for violating evacuating orders, was sentenced to five years probation in addition to being interned. Korematsu argued that it was not right to evacuate anyone without a hearing. Being an American citizen, he discovered, had little meaning for a Japanese-American.

In 1943 and 1944, the three cases were appealed to the United States Supreme Court which, in a series of unprecedented decisions, held that "military necessity" justified en masse racial evacuation and internment. The court based its findings of "military necessity" upon government representations that three persons of Japanese ancestry committed espionage and sabotage by signaling enemy ships from shore.

The Court also accepted government arguments that the loyalty of Japanese-Americans was suspect because of their racial characteristics. The Court, in its Hirabayashi decision wrote: "We cannot reject as unfounded the judgment of the military authorities and that of Congress that there were disloyal members of the Japanese-American population whose number and strength could not be ascertained."

The allegations of espionage, sabotage and disloyalty were contained in an official document entitled the *Final Report: Japanese Evacuation from the West Coast 1942*, written by Colonel Bendetsen. During this time he was directing the evacuation and internment ordered and signed by General John DeWitt. It is not unusual that the Supreme Court used this report since it was repeated verbatim in the court briefs of the Justice Department and the Attorney General of California, Oregon and Washington. Interestingly, the Final Report copied, without noting its source was used word for word in an earlier testimony given by Attorney General Earl Warren before congresssional committees in February 1942.

From the time, these Supreme Court decisions were written and filed in 1943, legal scholars have repeatedly criticized them for their inconsistencies and for direct opposition to accepted legal principles. One of the first and most convincing criticisms is found in Justice Frank Murphy's sharp dissenting opinion in the Korematsu case, which denounced the factual evidence presented by the Justice Department and accepted by his fellow justices. The evidence used to justify the evacuation was, he wrote, "largely an accumulation of much of the misinformation, half-truths and insinuations that for years have been directed against Japanese Americans by people who have been among the foremost advocates of the evacuation."

The Federal Commission on the Wartime Relocation and Internment of Civilians (CWRIC), forty years later reached the same conclusion as Justice Murphy. In its report entitled, Personal Justice Denied, the Commission stated: ". . . .the record does not permit the conclusion that military necessity warranted the exclusion of ethnic Japanese from the West Coast."

Petition for Writ of Error Coram Nobis

Some of the most important evidence presented at CWRIC hearings which supports their conclusion that no military necessity existed was developed and presented by Peter Irons, an attorney and professor of political science. Professor Irons; research of the War Department records in the National Archives led him to conclude that the government's evidence used in the three cases to justify the evacuation and internment was not only insufficient, but was purposely misleading and even falsified evidence!

Professor Irons contacted other attorneys working on the Wartime cases, as the Korematsu, Hirabayashi, and Yasui cases became commonly known, and together they formed a legal team to represent the three men in their efforts to reopen their cases and have their convictions reversed.

Each of the three men filed an identical Petition for Writ of Error Coram Nobis in the United States District Court in which he was originally convicted for violations of the evacuation and internment orders: Fred Korematsu in San Francisco, Gordon Hirabayashi in Seattle and Minoru Yasui in Portland.

Each man claimed that new evidence had been discovered which is sufficient for the court to grant his petition in order to prevent a grave injustice and to correct fundamental errors that affected the validity of the legal proceedings in which his conviction was upheld.

The three petitioners specifically claimed that the facts uncovered by Professor Irons showed:

1. That War Department officials altered and destroyed evidence and withheld knowledge of such actions from the Department of Justice and the Supreme Court.

2. That War and Justice Department officials suppressed evidence relative to the loyalty of Japanese-Americans and alleged acts of espionage.
3. That government officials failed to advise the Supreme Court of the falsity of the allegation made in General DeWitt's Final Report.
4. That the government's abuse of the doctrine of judicial notice and the manipulation of Amicus Briefs constituted a fraud upon the courts.
5. That the three petitioners were additionally entitled to relief on the ground that their convictions were based upon governmental orders and Constitutional standard that violated current Constitutional standards.

On November 10, 1983, Judge Marilyn Patel of the San Francisco Federal District Court, ruled that there was no factual basis for the original decision in the Korematsu case, found in Fred Korematsu's favor and vacated his conviction.

In part, Judge Patel ruled as she did because the Justice Department, did not file any meaningful response in behalf of the federal government. In effect, the government still had not admitted that any wrong had been committed against Japanese-Americans in early 1945 and will continue to fight the Hirabayashi and Yasui cases.

The judge, who reviewed the Hirabayashi case in Seattle, decided that the case was of such importance to merit a full court trial. This has forced the Justice Department to prepare and file a more meaningful response if it inteneded to continue to fight the cases or to admit formally that the petitioners' charges were correct, thus admitting that the government was wrong.

The Hirabayashi retrial has been set to be heard in June 1985. Many people who have been working so hard in behalf of the petitioners are looking forward to the exciting prospect that the wartime cases will finally be overturned!

Internees in World War II Can Sue

In a suit brought by 19 Japanese-Americans, a three-judge panel of the U.S. Circuit Court of Appeals in the District of Columbia overruled District *Judge Louis F. Oberdorfer,* who held in

1984 that the federal statue of limitations barred Japanese-Americans from making any claims against the United States government after six years. The panel voted 2-1 to reverse the old ruling.

This will allow Japanese-Americans interned during World War II to sue for as much as $24 billion in damages.

Judge J. Skelly Wright, who wrote the decision for the panel, declared the statutory limit is irrelevant in this special case. The government has admitted in other cases, Wright stated, the Justice Department's concealment of evidence showing that the confinement of all Japaneses-Americans during World War II was not necessary to preserve the national security.

"Extraordinary injustice can prove extraordinary acts of concealment," Wright noted. "Where such concealment is alleged, it ill-behooves the government of a free people to evade an honest accounting."

One of the plaintiffs, *George Ikeda 65,* said, "I'm glad that justice at least will get to court. I'm glad that they will hear our case. Justice should be done. I figured that I should let everybody know what happened to us at that time." Ikeda was interned in Poston, Arizona.

Reverend Kyoshiro Tokunaga, 80, another internee and a Buddhist priest, was interned at camps in Santa Fe and Lordsburg, New Mexico.

"It's getting too late," he said, "Most of the people who suffered are going rapidly. I don't know how long it will take for the government to clear this thing. But at the rate they have been going, I think most of the people who have suffered the most will be gone in no time. It is more of a moral issue than a monetary one."

Harry Ueno, 78, who was at Manzanar in Southern California, stated of the ruling, "That's beautiful. We're going to continue to press on to get the favor to our decision."

William Hohri, a former Californian prior to his incarceration, now a Chicago computer programmer, agrees with Reverend Tokunaga that he, too, as well many internees are interested not so much in the monetary gains, but in the court's ruling that their constitutional rights had been violated.

Hohri estimates that the average claim will reach a range of approximately $200,000. (The U.S. government had placed approximately 120,000 Japanese and Japanese-Americans in concentration camps for a duration of about three years.)

Susan Hayase, Chair of the San Jose (California) based Japanese American Outreach Committee, one of the founding organizations of the National Coalition for Redress and Reparations said, "The reinstating of the suit is a real victory. . . . This is an issue that has been long-standing and long overdue. Over 40 years overdue."

Congress has passed enabling laws to partially compensate interned Japanese-Americans in the 1950's for property seized, and in 1986 Congress is reviewing legislation to provide an automatic $20,000 for each of some 66,000 survivors of the relocation camps. This later bill, HR 442, would also make a formal apology for confinement and the establish an educational foundation for Japanese Americans.

Congressman Robert T. Masui, D. California, said he and *Congressman Norman Y. Mineta,* D California are pressing for passage of this bill, which presently has 120 co-sponsors. Both Matsui and Mineta had been interned during the war years of 1942-1945.

"The bill, [HR 442], would not put people in an adversarial position against the government, having to prove their losses," Matsui said. By contrast, he stated, those seeing redress through the courts would be required to submit evidence of damage as a result of their confinement.

Mineta, hailing the appeals court's decision, stated: The court "recognized that an unusual response is necessary to this tragedy. As the court said, those who suffered injustice should be free to press this case to its conclusion. Now that statute of limitations problem has been set aside, we can have our day in court and present the facts which for far too long have been hidden from review."[25]

Chapter 9
CHALLENGE

Is Bigotry and Racial Prejudice
Rising Again in California?

There seems to be evidence that bigotry and racial prejudice is again being exercised by not only the media, but by blue collar workers who either lost jobs from the automobile industries and other manufacturers or heads of companies providing goods or services in direct competition with Japan. These biases or racial innuendoes are being created by placing ads in newspapers, racial caricatures and verbal public messages against Japan by prominent private and public leaders in our country.

Historically, these subtle, yet effective propaganda, when exercised on a continual basis with or without a "Madison Avenue" approach will eventually have its toll and will create unreasonable "built in prejudice" which can escalate into an almost rational "get hate" program. Similar continual campaign and attention were exercised during the period of 1860-1940 by the California agriculturalists as well as organizations such as the Native Sons and Daughters of the Golden West and other racist and hate groups (of that era) whose sole purpose was to remove a targeted segment of an American society only because of the color of their skin. The same scenario of the past is surfacing.

Again in 1985, there is evidence that these very same subtle "hate campaigns" are being orchestrated by corporate media echoing the same kind of dialogue which are reminiscent of the 1860-

1940 era. Today, the traditional voices of anti-Japanese agitation are being energetically endorsed by the economic competitors of Japan. Yet due to these subtle tactics in their plea for "unfair internationaal trade competition", the average American is not cognizant of the fact that their racial tactics against Japan may once again refocus on Japanese-Americans becoming not only the "scapegoat" but also the artificial cause for the demise of those affected by Japan's aggressive trade program. History tends to repeat itself. The Grower-Shipper Vegetable Association bluntest statement can be found in a Saturday Evening Post article in May, 1942:

"We're charged with wanting to get rid of Japs for selfish reasons. We might as well be honest. We do. It's a question of whether the white man lives on the Pacific Coast or the brown man. They came into this valley to work, and they stayed to take over. . . . If all the Japs were removed tomorrow, we'd never miss them in two weeks, because the white farmers can take over and produce everything the Jap grows. And we don't want them back when the war ends, either."[26]

The Bigotry Bug is Catching Again

Columnist H. Bruce Miller writes that bigotry in California is going strong and doing as well as the economy of Silicon Valley (Santa Clara County). When we talk about California, we conjure up images of suntans, surfboards, Rose Bowl queens and earthquakes. This tradition of hate and bigotry started before the gold rush, and even after a century a half, in the middle of the "Silicon Rush," racism and bigotry are still going strong.

Yet, the direction and targets have shifted after a century and a half from the Chinese or the Japanese being the main focus of attack. The new candidates for this attack are the Southeast Asian refugees, the quarter-million or so people who fled to California from Vietnam, Laos and Cambodia.

In a recent interview with executive director of the Santa Clara County Human Relations Commission, Jim McEntee, whose job it is to spot the disaster of bigotry early as possible and stopping it before it becomes an epidemic, stated that the symptoms are subtle and scattered now, yet they're unmistakably there. McEntee gave an incident of a refugee family's windows being bro-

105

ken, a car trashed, and a a fight at a high school which might be racially related. "We're picking up vibes from the schools that the school situation is tense," McEntee says. He has a son in Independence High School (San Jose, California) and "he's mentioned hearing terms like 'nips,' 'flips,' and 'chinks.' Jees, I haven't heard those things since the late '40s."

Many incidents such as the attacks on 31 Laotian families living on San Jose's East Side who had had their car tires slashed in one night although reported to the police, seldom get reported in local newspapers since minor incidents such as these are not normally newsworthy. It is further noted, that since the Laotians are quiet and not very visible, most minor incidents are not reported to the proper authorities, due to the victims' fear of reprisal of their language barrier.

At the core of the bigot's thought process, or what passes for one, is a kind of unfocused economic resentment and expressions of negative comments which is similar to the subtle innuendoes and fear against the Japanese-Americans, during the 1860-1940 era which eventually led to the proper rational for their exclusion from the West Coast during the World War II duration.

"I think people have taken the economic situation and the competition from imports and applied it in a general way," McEntee says. "That's another thing we do—we lump all Asians together. We take the Asians and say, "It's their fault I'm out of a job."

This resentment fueled by envy takes on a more direct and personal form. Those affected see individual refugees as taking jobs from American workers. If they see refugees owning their own businesses, this further adds to their resentment because now their ego are being taxed.

"I've had some people from other ethnic groups say, you know, "how in the heck did these people do it?", McEntee says. "Where do they get the money? How do they start a business?" My response to them is: "Why don't you go ask them? Because I know how they're able to do it: They're willing to work long hours and run a family operation so they're not paying outside help. They're willing to take a cut for a good long time in order to have a business."

Paul Arnold, director of the Refugee Project of the San Jose Metropolitan Adult Education Program, which trains refugees for a variety of jobs such as silicon wafer fabricators to nurse's aides, states that employers hire his graduates as quickly as the program can train them.

There's no mystery why, he adds: "They're very punctual, they're very conscientious, they're hard workers, they'll take any job"—including low-paid jobs that many Americans scorn.

"The thinking of bigots doesn't seem to change much no matter what the era or the target. The Chinese or Mexicans or Laotians or whoever are put in a damned-if-they-do, damned-if they-don't position. If they go on welfare, they're sponging off the taxpayers. If they get jobs, work hard and succeed, then they're taking what 'rightfully' belongs to Americans."

"There's a contorted logic to all this—not the logic of the brain, but the logic of the gut, the logic of fear and jealousy. These people with their funny languages and outlandish customs come over here and do a better job of realizing the American dream then many Americans do. Their success is an implicit reproach. The bigot hates because hating is easier than admitting the truth of the reproach."

In 1984, McEntree's Human Relations Commission heard testimony from more than forty individuals and groups who shared their perceptions about prejudices against Southeast Asians. The Commission is presently reviewing all of this evidence and will make policy recommendations to governments of all levels. Although this seems to be a commendable effort by the Commission, legislation alone by government will have little or no effect unless its citizens, individually realize that the roots of the problem are twisted deep in the human psyche and in our culture.

"One thing we've got going for us is that along with its tradition of bigotry, California has another tradition just as old and far more honorable—the tradition of giving the other guy an even break, of letting him go as far as his talents and labor can take him, of judging him not by where he came from, but by what he can do. And when you look at history, you see that in the long run, tradition usually wins."[27]

Spirit Week—Homestead High School

The following is a news article and a letter to the editor on the unfortunate incident that occurred at a middle class, California high school in Santa Clara County, during their Spirit Week in

107

October, 1984.

The Epitaph, a school newspaper of the Homestead High School, Cupertino, California, featured "Vacation Spots," the theme of the 1984's Homecoming Week.

The Sophomore Spirit Day focused on Japan as their theme. Assistant Principal Peter Tuana stated: "Although enthusiasm was strong, not everyone was happy with Spirit Week. Some of the posters hung during Sophomore Spirit Day were taken down. Anything done out of taste was taken care of," he concluded.

Sophomore Brad Wong was offended. Derogatory posters and racial cartoons were offensive and are totally uncalled for, Wong stated.

Following this incident, Brad Wong, responded with a letter to the Editor:

Dear Epitaph:

I am writing to you concerning Sophomore Spirit Day and its treatment. First, I must commend the efforts of the sophomore class officers and other students who put spirit day together, but I must protest the way Japan and the Japanese people were presented. The Japanese were typecasted, shown in many negative stereotypes, and were shown with non-flattering and degrading ways. Many of the students dressed up as tourists, with cameras and floral print shirts.

True, many Japanese are tourists and in my opinion this idea was only picked because many Homestead students could relate with them as being tourists, but this depicted the Japanese as 'stupid' tourists. Isn't there more to Japan and its culture than a camera and a floral print shirt? Also many Japanese-Americans dressed up as tourists toting around their camera and mimicking the tourist's "choppy" English. These students were making fun of their culture and heritage as if it were a game, and it just proved the racial awareness is not everywhere.

I don't understand why rice was thrown. Was someone getting married? I wonder if Americans throw hamburgers. Another disturbing scene was during brunch and lunch when students began to mimic, mock, and imitate the Japanese by saying racist remarks. At brunch, my friend was confronted by a person who said, "Happy Nip Day."

Other racial slurs such as "ah-so", the popular "choppy English," and other uninterpretable sayings were common by the end of the day.

Posters, banners, and slogans were also degrading. Posters such as "Wok's up Doc?"; "Watch out Pearl Harbor, here we come!"; "What kind of car do you drive?"; "Nip, nip, hurray"; "It's getting nippy out there," and cartoons with slanted eyes and buck teeth were offensive and totally uncalled for.

Japan was a very narrow idea and controversial issue. Ideas such as the Cherry Blossom Festival and having a taiko drum group perform were overlooked. The class officers and the sophomore students walked a fine line from things that could be taken offensively and from things that have spirit. From what I witnessed today, they crossed that line. I don't think the officers and class members purposely tried to offend anyone, but they didn't realize many of the things they were doing were considered racist and insensitive. A large percent of Asians go to Homestead and there should have been more consideration for their feelings as well as others. The sophomore class has to be an unenlightened group of students; should learn from this experience today, and I can say ignorance is alive and well as Homestead.[28]

Racism Implicated in Fatal Stabbing of Student

Thong Hy Huynh, a Vietnamese student, attending Davis High School, near Sacramento, California, in May, 1983, was fatally stabbed to death by James Pierman, a white fellow school mate. Pierman, 16 at the time of the killing, is being tried as an adult.

Testifying through an interpreter, Duc Nguyen, a close friend and a former classmate of Huynh said that he and three other Vietnamese students had been the target of racial taunts for at least three weeks before the stabbing.

Nguyen told the jury that he and his three friends were walking back to classes after lunch when they were confronted by Pierman and Russell Clark. Nguyen said he ignored Clark's challenge to fight until Clark pushed him and then hit him in the mouth. Pierman, he said, had been "holding a knife and waving it."

At one point, Nguyen said he was hit in the eye and knocked to the ground. "I couldn't see anything. The first thing I realized when I opened my eyes was that Thong was lying on the ground. I thought he was just unconscious," he recalled.

Nguyen choked up and had to pause in his testimony as he talked about trying to help Huynh, who was mortally wounded from a single knife wound to the heart.

"He (Pierman) took out the knife and waved it in front of our faces," said Bon Chau, another Vietnamese student involved in the fight. "Then he put the knife back in the sleeve of his shirt and said to the fat guy (Clark), "You go ahead and hit one of them. If they hit you, I will use the knife." Both Chau and Nguyen testified that they did not actually see Pierman thrust the knife into Huynh.

Defense attorney William Maas said that Huynh accidentally fell on the knife during the fight, and that Pierman immediately used his shirt to try and stop the bleeding saying, "It was an accident. I didn't mean to do it."

Jurors, however, listened to a tape of Pierman's statements to the police shortly after the incident. The statements, asserted the prosecution, contradict what the defendant now says happened at the time of the stabbing.

"Two things that were pointed out during the testimony were that Pierman used a lot of "F"' words toward the Vietnamese students and derogatory words relating to their being Vietnamese and from Vietnam," said Diane Tomoda, a spokesperson for the Coalition of Asians for Equal Rights.

District Attorney David Henderson said that Pierman kept an ax, a large knife, a smaller knife, and a baseball bat in his car, all of which he needed for "the people who crossed his path."

On October 1, 1984, after a week of deliberation, a jury convicted James "Jay" Pierman, of voluntary manslaughter for the stabbing death of Thong Hy Huynh at Davis High School in May, 1983.

Criminal attorney Garrick Lew of San Francisco stated that Pierman could receive three, six or eleven years in the state prison. Pierman could receive a mitigated sentence of three years if he had no previous convictions, but according to a Davis newspaper, he has five previous arrests, including battery charges.

"Racial motivation might have to be considered," said Lew. "The judge can also take public sentiment into consideration if he receives a number of negative letters about the crime Pierman committed."[29]

The focus will be on whether or not the stabbing was deliberate. Pierman's attorney, William Maas insisted that it was an accident. After the verdict, he said that his client "felt bad" about the outcome and had been hoping for an acquittal or conviction for involuntary manslaughter.

Pierman did not testify, but a tape of his statements shortly after his arrest indicated hostility toward Vietnamese people, one observer said.

Justice Demanded in Race-Related "Murder" of Vincent Chin

Asians from various community groups throughout the country have banded together in Los Angeles, California to protest the handling of the Vincent Chin murder. Joining them, were high political figures from both local and state levels as well as the general public who rallied and displayed an unprecedented solidarity to this cause.

"The Vincent Chin case has generated the most interest from around the United States of any case—any civil rights case—of this present administration," said Assistant Attorney General William Bradford Reynolds, head of the Justice Department's Civil Rights Division. In all my cases, I have never seen so much public or political pressure as in this case."

Vincent Chin, the victim in the case, was an American of Chinese ancestry who was beaten to death with a baseball bat in Detroit on June 19, 1982, by two auto workers who blamed him for the unemployment of Americans. (It is proported, that Ronald Ebens and Michael Nitz mistook Chin to be "Japanese".)

This case has taken national attention due the fact that not only was Chin stalked and assaulted in a manner which many consider pre-meditated, eventually leading to his death, but that the motive behind his murder has racial overtones.

In a previous court decision, Wayne County Circuit Judge Kaufman accepted the manslaughter plea and released Ebens and Nitz with a $3,000 one and three year probation, respectively, which many think to be too light of a sentence.

Secretary of State March Fong Eu and Los Angeles Mayor Tom Bradley demanded that federal charges be filed. "We will not

111

stand silently by and permit this incident to be forgotten," Bradley said. "We will call upon the attorney general of the United States because if this government stands for anything, it must stand for justice."

"We insist that the murderers of Vincent Chin receive their day in court to be truly judged and punished by the same standards applied to other murderers," said Eu. "We insist that the U.S. Department of Justice file charges and prosecute these perpetrators of this heinous act against humanity."

Mrs. Lily Chin (mother of the late Vincent Chin) rose to speak. In a stoic solemn voice she stated (translated from Chinese by Dr. Marisa Chuang): "I want justice for my son. What happened to him could happen to any of us. We cannot let the killers (be) free on probation—we cannot allow the justice system do whatever they want. If we do, where is there justice? If we do, where do we have protection?

"I promise you, that as long a I live, I will want to do whatever I can so that no other mother will suffer what I have gone through. I will work hard for justice and I appeal to all of you to continue our quest for justice for all."

As Mrs. Chin completed her remarks, Dr. Chuang offered that there are two ways of obtaining justice for Chin.

"If there is evidence of racism in the killing then there will be a federal case." She said if the killers are found guilty, they would be subjected to life imprisonment.

"There is no question in our minds that racism killed Vincent Chin," said March Fong Eu. "The most fitting tribute to him and his family and to his mother is to dedicate ourselves to insuring that he kills no other," the Secretary of State said.

Art Snyder, Los Angeles councilman, presented Mrs. Chin with a resolution from the City of Los Angeles. "On the 21st (June, 1984), I presented this Resolution (and) the City Council not only adopted it unanimously but five members rose to speak in support of the Resolution."

The Resolution

". . . Throughout the nation, Americans have rallied in protest to this gross miscarraige of justice, which carries within it a challenge to the rule of law and the human rights guaranteed by our Constitution and the laws of the land. City councils, county boards of supervisors, and state legislatures are joining in the demand for further federal action in the Chin case.

"I therefore move that the City Council of the City of Los Angeles join with the State of California in petitioning the Attorney General of the United States to commence an investigation into the murder of Vincent Chin and the events preceding and following it, and should it appear that the laws of the United States of America have been violated, then to prosecute his murderers to the extent that the law allows.[29]

(A federal civil suit under the Federal Civil Rights Act has been initiated in Detroit on this cases. Ebens was sentenced on September 18, 1984 to twenty-five years in prison and is expected to appeal the sentence.)

Racial Caricatures

Not Offensive?

The following caricature is a poster at Six Flags, Auto World at Flint, Michigan. Flint is a major auto manufacturing city, and Fisher Body Divison of General Motors is its major employer.

One of the theme park's exhibits, entitled "Life, Courtesy of Automoble," includes a poster showing a flying car with such caricatured features as buck teeth and slits for eye—"reminiscent of World War II propaganda art"—bombing an aircraft carrier labeled "Detroit" with Japan's wartime flag forming the background.

Helen Zia, president of American Citizens for Justice, stated: "We feel that there is no place for such racist displays, and certainly not where children and visitors to our state can be influenced by such propaganda. This kind of racial sterotyping encourages the kind of antagonism that led to the racially motivated attack and killing of Vincent Chin . . ."

Prosecution witnesses on the trial of Ronald Eben (Vincent Chin case) stated the former auto worker Ebens used racial slurs and blamed Asians for the poor economic state of the auto industry.

Six Flags public relations manager Kathy Schoch dismissed the

PLATE 5 31

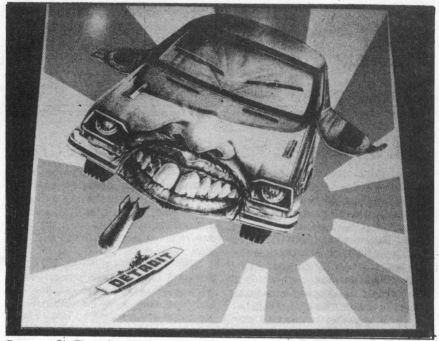

Poster at Six Flags Auto World, Flint, Mich.   Photo courtesy: Pacific Citizen

charges of racism, saying: . . . "that the poster is no more offensive than others in the exhibit. A poster done in pink might be seen as depicting homosexuals, while a used-car salesman in a loud plaid coat with a large nose might be taken as a Jew."[30]

Promotion of a National Trade Policy

President Ronald Reagan has been criticized on not taking a more active role as President regarding the imbalance in the international trade and a definite stand. It is purported that President Reagan had made only two speeches regarding international trade policies. One as President in 1984, and the latter one when he was Governor of the State of California . . . Reagan recounted one of his stories: . . . "driving down California highway" . . . while as governor . . . and seeing "Buy American" bumper sticker on a Toyota. "That," he said, "ended the discussion on trade policies."

Trade Protectionists' Singling Out Japan

Senators Lloyd Bentsen of Texas and Richard Gephardt of Missouri are writing the final details in the 1985 Congress, a bill to slap a twenty-percent tariff on all imports from Japan, unless the Japanese show by declining trade surpluses, that they formally open their home market to goods from abroad. These legislators by singling out only Japan (not other European nations having similar trade barriers) as the "problem", again raises the questions by civil rights observers whether these senators are only racially biased rather than concerned about trade inequity practices by many nations.

Again, caricatures as noted below, focusing on Japan being portrayed as the "bad guy," may cause undue injustice and racism in the near future.[32]

PLATE 6[32]

Sandra Tanaka

Japan view down the gun barrel!

Pearl Harbor Party

This particular cartoon advertisement was placed in the San Jose State University's Spartan Daily . . . on December 7, 1984. Even this so-called innocent isolated racial situation ad as noted in Plate 4, all points out that even after more than forty years

116

after World War II, propaganda and innocent sounding statements are still being advanced which may again nurture public opinion that will approve the incarceration of Japanese and Japanese American citizens, or other ethnic Americans. It is evident that the present day intellectual college students are not understanding the insensitivities they are promoting.[33]

PLATE 8

Racism on the Road?   Sandra Tanaka

Racism on the Road?
This caricature sketched was recently spotted in the window of a car parked in Los Angeles. Its apparent message is depicting the Chinese or Vietnamese (or Asians) are poor drivers and should be banned from the road. Another explanation for this may be that Japanese should be ostracized since they are creating a major impact on the American economy due to their aggressive importation of their autos. (It could not be determined whether the picture was hand-drawn or pre-printed commercial label.)

117

Iacocca's "Nationalism"

Lee Iacocca, Chairman of the Board of Chrysler Corporation, delivered a speech on United States trade policy to a gathering of Democratic congressmen in early March 1985. In his speech, he singled out only Japan as the "problem," although other European governments also have protectionist trade policies.

This action, again, historically suggests that certain special interest groups, organizations and corporations by singling out Japan, not "white" European countries for creating possible economic impacts, may again, provide the rational for the racial hatred against Japan, which will ultimately turn once again upon Japanese-Americans or other "yellow-skinned citizens" of the United States, due to ethnicity alone.

Considering the irresponsible action of Iacocca singling out a particular group of people as the "problem," Congressman Mike Lowry (D. Washington) wrote a letter to Mr. Iacocca and stated in part: "Because of your tone of zealous nationalism, specifically in addressing the actions of the Japanese . . .

"I am confident that this was not your intention. However, there is nothing easier than arousing a strong response when a particular people are singled out as the cause of the problem.

"Your address would have been even more powerful and instructive had you clarified that you were addressing the trade policies of the Japanese government and corporations, and not the Japanese people as a whole.

"It would have added to your speech to note that many European governments have equally protectionist trade policies.

"I have a tremendous regard for the leadership you have shown at Chrysler and in the United States business community. I know you are aware of the destruction which has resulted from base appeals to nationalism in our own nation and abroad.

"I am simply concerned that rhetorical appeals to our lesser instincts move us no closer to addressing our very real trade imbalance problem, nor does it reflect well on us as a nation."[34]

Chapter 10
UNFINISHED AGENDA—REDRESS

Pending Redress Bill

My father had said: "I understand, Congressmen Norman Mineta and Robert Matsui, Senators Inouye and Masunaga are pushing the $20,000 redress bill." "Will it soon pass?" I stated that there is great support and enthusiasm for the bill. My father stated: "I don't think I will see this bill pass in my lifetime." I told my father to hang on, I think you will see it. I asked my father what was the importance of this legislature as he saw it. He stated: "Although it is important to many of us to receive this money, since we lost most of our finances due to the war, yet I feel grateful that we were able to educate you children and live a reasonable free and happy life. What is important is the principle. I believe America made a mistake. I am a Nisei American citizen, uprooted in my prime; had to give up my livelihood; sent to concentration camp for no reason; and then after our return, we had to start all over again. Many of us didn't make it! This is a small token America should make for the thousands of broken lives. Son, this is only fair, this is only fair."

My father realizing that he was getting old, approximately 80 years old, empathized for the 60,000 Japanese and Japanese-Americans who have passed away prior to the passage of any redress in the United States Congress. He stated: "Your grandfather, grandmother, and mother have passed on. How many more will be gone before an apology be given by the government?"

Reviewing the many versions of the pending legislation on redress in Congress, my father stated: "Son I may not live to see this bill pass." I assured him, "You are only near 80 years old, hang on, and you will see it." Father was right. He will not see any redress bills passed in his lifetime. He died in July, 1983, one of 60,000 of the 120,000 Japanese and Japanese-Americans incarcerated in American concentration camps who had passed on without any apology from the United States of America.

Redress legislation by October 16, 1984 is being backed by 106 representatives and twenty senators. Although this number does not represent a clear majority in either house, one can speculate the support will increase after the public understands the essence of these bills.

The National Coalition for Redress/Reparations

U.S. Concentration Camps

On February 19, 1942, President Franklin D. Roosevelt signed Executive Order 9066, authorizing the mass evacuation and incarceration of 120,000 Japanese-Americans. Almost two-thirds of those interned were citizens born and raised in the United States who never set foot in Japan. The remaining internees were permanent residents of the U.S. who had left Japan at least seventeen years earlier and had remained Japanese nationals, because citizenship was denied them through discriminatory U.S. naturalization laws.

According to the Munson Report, commissioned by the U.S. government and completed in early 1942, stated that the Japanese-Americans were considered unquestionably loyal to the United States. Without evidence of wrongdoing, specific charges, or due process of law, citizens and permanent residents alike were publically branded as "the enemy," "disloyal," or "traitors." As a consequence, they lost property, homes, savings, income, businesses, and other sources of income. They were also denied intangibles such as health, freedom, and dignity, all supposedly guaranteed by the Constitution and other means of protection of human and civil rights in the United States. The U.S. government, under the guise of "military necessity" justified the racist imprisonment of Japanese-Americans. However, no such roundup of German or Italian-Americans occurred. For approximately the next three years, Japanese-Americans lived behind barbed wires under armed military guard. The ten concentration camps were located in the most desolate and remote areas of the United States. Aside from what was carried in by hand, all personal possessions were lost; bank accounts were frozen; educational and career opportunities were disrupted; and cultural and community ties were destroyed.

The proposal to remove Japanese-Americans and separate them from the rest of society was actively supported by many of the groups which backed earlier discriminatory policies. In this sense, the forced internment into concentration camps was the most devastating blow among a long series of measures against Japanese-Americans.

It has taken more than forty years for the Japanese-Americans to sufficiently recover their dignity to build a redress movement. The Commission on Wartime Relocation and Internment of Civilians authorized by Congress has responded to the demand for redress by the Japanese-Americans. In addition to seeking a formal admission of wrong doing by the government, reparation through legislation is also being sought.

1983 Commission on Wartime Relocation and Internment of Civilians' Recommendation

By an Act of Congress in 1980, a Commission was established to:

1. Review the facts and circumstances surrounding Executive Order 9066, and the impact of that Order on American citizens and permanent residents aliens;
2. Review directives of the United States military forces requiring the relocation and detention and recommend appropriate remedies.

Following this mandate, the Commission on Wartime Relocation and Internment of Civilians carried out its investigations and research over a two and one-half year period. It included twenty hearing days and the taking of testimony of 750 witnesses which included evacuees, former government officials, public figures, interested citizens, historians and other professionals who had studied the subject. It also made a thorough and extensive review of records and documents, some of which had only become available recently.

The Commission on Wartime Relocation and Internment of Civilians concluded their hearings in 1983 and published their recommendations. The redress bills authored by Senators Cranston and Matsunaga and Representatives Wright and Lowry include many of the (CWRIC) findings. Below is a summary of the (CWRIC) recommendations, of June 1983;

1. That Congress pass a joint resolution which recognizes that a grave injustice was done and offer the apologies of the nation.
2. That the President pardon those who were convicted of violating the statutes imposing a curfew and requiring the ethnic Japanese to leave designated areas or to report to assembly centers. That the Department of Justice review other wartime convictions and recommend to the President that he pardon those whose offenses were founded in a refusal to accept treatment that discriminated among citizens on the basis of race and ethnicity.
3. That Congress direct the executive agencies to which Japanese-Americans may apply for the restitution of positions, status or entitlements lost in whole or in part because of acts or events between December '41 and '45 to review such applications with liberality. For example, the Department of Defense should review cases of less than honorable discharge of Japanese-Americans from the armed services during World War II over which disputes remain, and the Commission of Social Security should review any remaining complaints of inequity in entitlements due to the wartime detention.
4. That Congress establish a special foundation to sponsor research and public educational activities so that the events, causes and circumstances of evaluation, relocation and internment be remembered and understood.
5. That Congress establish a fund to provide personal redress of $20,000 to each of the surviving 60,000 persons who were excluded due to Executive Order 9066 as well as serve the purposes in Recommendation 4. Appropriation of $1.5 billion should be made to the fund over a

reasonable period to be determined by Congress. Oldest survivors should be compensated first with the burden of locating survivors to be the government's. That the remainder of the fund be used to carry out Recommendation 4 as well as used for the general welfare of the Japanese-Americans community. This fund shall be administered by a board, the majority of whose members would be Nikkei.

The Commission made the following recommendations in regard to the Aleuts:

1. That Congress establish a fund of $5 million for beneficial use of the Aleuts such as community educational, cultural or historical rebuilding in addition to medical or social services.
2. That Congress appropriate funds to pay $5,000 to each of the surviving Aleuts who were evacuated.
3. That Congress appropriate funds to rebuild and restore churches damaged or destroyed in the Aleutian Island in the course of World War II and that preference in employment of such be given to Aleuts.
4. That Congress appropriate funds for the Army Corps of Engineers to clear away the World War II debris and remains in and around the populated areas of the Aleutian Islands.
5. That Congress declare Attu to be native land and returned to the Aleuts.

Finally, the Commission recommended that a permanent collection be established and funded in the National Archives to house and make available for research, the government and private documents, testimonies and other materials of the CWRIC.

Four Redress Bills:

The Differences
Four redress bills were introduced in Congress in 1983. Two by the Senators Cranston and Matsunaga and two in the House by Representatives Wright and Lowry.

SB 1520—"World War II Civil Liberties Violations Redress Act" introduced by Senator Alan Cranston in June—. This bill, in a very broad sense, supports the Commission on the Wartime Relocation and Internment of Civilians (CWRIC) recommendations. Differences: a) Does not specify a dollar amount, leaving that matter to be decided by Congress. b) Redress all those who were interned, not just survivors, with payments for those already deceased to go into the trust fund. c) Calls for direct payments while CWRIC recommends the establishing a trust fund—first out of which payments would be made. d) Payments be made within three years of enactment of the bill.

HR 3387—"World War II Civil Liberties Violation Redress Act" introduced by Rep. Mike Lowry in June—this bill approximates CWRIC recommendations. Differences: a) Provides $20,000 to Aleuts. b) States that internees be located and redressed within a year of enactment of the bill.

HR 4110—"Civil Liberties Act of 1983" introduced by House Majority Leader Jim Wright in October—Endorses CWRIC recommendations.

SB 2116—Introduced by Senator Spark Matsunaga in November. Accepts the findings and asks for the implementation of the CWRIC recommendations. Difference: a) Provides for $12,000 to Aleuts.

1983 Commission on Wartime Relocation and Internment of Civilians
Honorable Judge Wayne Kanemoto

The bipartisan nine member Commission made its unanimous final report to Congress in February, 1983, concluding:

> "that personal justice was denied that the 1942 rationale of "military necessity" had no basis in fact; and that the causes of the internment were "race prejudice, war hysteria, and failure of political leadership."

The Commission's chairperson, Joan Z. Bernstein, in reporting to a Congressional Committee stated: "No amount of money can fully compensate the excluded people for their losses and suffering. Two and one-half years behind barbed wire of a relocation camp, branded potentially disloyal because of one's ethnicity alone—these injustices cannot be neatly turned into dollars and cents. . . . History cannot be undone; anything we do now must inevitable be an expression of regret and an affirmation of our better values as a nation, not an accounting which balances or erases the events of the war. That is now beyond anyone's power."

But the report went on: "It is well within our power, however, to provide remedies for violations of our own laws and principles. This is one important reason for the several forms of redress recommended.

Another is that our nation's ability to honor democratic values even in times of stress depends largely upon our collective memory of lapses from our constitutional committment to liberty and due process. Nations that forget or ignore injustices are more likely to repeat them.

Our legal system is founded on determining guilt or fault on an individual basis, and the conclusion that ethnicity determined loyalty was not a military judgment deserving of any credence. Generals are not experts on race: their views on the political loyalties of civilians are only as good as the facts they can marshal in their support.

As John J. McCloy, who was Assistant Secretary of War in 1942, testified to the Commission, the decision to issue the exclusion order was not based on any actual events of sabotage or espionage known to the War Department. The lack of evidence of disloyalty on the part of Americans of Japanese ancestry in 1942 speaks for itself.

By any analysis with the least sensitivity to American constitutional values, there was no justification for holding loyal American citizens of Japanese descent in detention or prohibiting them from traveling, living and working where they chose.

In his memoirs, Secretary of War Henry L. Stimson cogently called the evacuation a 'personal injustice" to loyal Americans. It was a personal injustice precisely because the country failed to apply justice in a personal individual manner.

It is important to emphasize that we are dealing here with American behavior. It is not a question of how the Japanese or the Nazis treated Americans or other prisoners. . . . What the Commission has examined and taken testimony about . . . is how the United States dealt with American citizens and residents.

An essential foundation of our government—the citizen's trust that the government will deal with him or her individually and fairly—was deeply damaged.

Over time and with perserverance, material losses may be repaired but hidden scars of lives damaged by the exclusion and detention will remain.

For people who knew their innocence and the injustices of their treatment, the burden was not light. They bore the stigma of having been branded potentially disloyal, the deprivation of liberty, and loss of the common decencies of daily life.

The commissioners deplore the method and the record of Japan's armed forces during World War II, but it must be kept clearly in mind that the American citizens who were sent to Manzanar or Poston (or and other relocation center) were no more responsible for Pearl Harbor and the Bataan Death March than German-Americans were for the invasion of France or the bombing of Britain. (It appears the Commission chairman was politely omitting any reference to Auschwitz or Dachau.)

The American principle, that a man/women is judged as an individual and not by where his/her grandparents came from must not be allowed to become a casualty of war.

A free act of apology to those who were unjustly excluded and detained during the war is an important act of national healing. . . . If we are unwilling as a nation to apologize for these events, we will deliver a message to the thousands of loyal Americans who were held in the camps that will be bitter indeed.

We will be affirming after 40 years that the American values of due process and equality before the law without regard to ethnicity are only rhetorical values and that in times of stress small minorities should harbor no hope that those principles will protect them from fear and anger of their neighbors or the heavy hand of their government. Such a result is a threat to the liberty of all Americans.

In addressing monetary payments, two points must be borne in mind. First, the Commission was asked to recommend appropriate remedies, not simply ordinary and usual remedies. For events as usual and extraordinary as these, one can only expect an extraordinary response.

Second, the justification for monetary payments need not rest solely on an argument as to whether the initial acts of 1942 were totally unjustified. One need only look at the last 18 months of exclusion and detention.

By the middle of 1943, there was no conceivable threat of attack on the West Coast from Japan. Fifteen months of incarceration had provided ample time to identify spies and saboteurs if there were any of significance. Secretary Stimson and Mr. McCloy had concluded there was no military reasons justifying the exclusion of the loyal Japanese/Americans from the West Coast (after mid-1943).

Nevertheless, the Japanese-Americans were not allowed to go home until the end of 1944 and most of them spent that 30 months behind barbed wire.

It's hard to imagine circumstances more clearly of justifying compensation from the government.

The day following the report of the Commission's recommendations, there appeared a news article reporting the outcome of a jury trial in Southern California.

It appeared that a young lady had, years before, joined the Hare Krishna group but had quickly became disenchanted and decided to leave the group. However, she was forcibly detained for a period of time.

Sometime later apparently she did leave or escape and filed suit for damages against the Hare Krishna, which case had come to trial. The news article reported that the jury had awarded the young lady $3 million damages.

My immediate reaction was that if you must be kidnapped or falsely imprisoned, it should always be by the Hare Krishna or a similar group, never by your own Government, because in the latter you can expect, at best, only $20,000.

An American Tragedy, and Reparations
Congresssman Norman Y. Mineta

The internment. To many Americans, that phrase means little. But to more than 110,000 American citizens and law abiding residents, the internment meant years of imprisonment, impoverishment, and shame.

Americans of Japanese ancestry were evacuated and interned by the U.S. Army shortly after the United States entered World

War II. [In 1985,] several of us in Congress introduced the World War II Civil Liberties Violation Redress Act, which proposes compensation for each of the former internees who is still alive.

In February 1983 the Commisssion ended a year and a half of investigations with a report concluding that the internment was prompted not by the exigencies of national security, but by "hysteria," "racism," and a "failure of political leadership."

Three conclusions constitute the basic support for redress. First, the internment was not a necessary step in the defense of American security. Second, the internment involved the unjustified imprisonment of Americans. And third, redress involves the pursuit of equal justice rather than the arrangement of special advantage.

Why compensate those interned?

Some now shrug off the fact that Americans of Japanese ancestry never presented a threat to American security. They may concede that the internment was an ill-conceived action that caused unnecessary suffering. But they note, "We all suffered during the war."

Of course, America was at war. And as Americans, we all joined together to defend our country, and we all accepted the sacrifices that defense entailed. Indeed, Americans of Japanese ancestry contributed mightily to the Allied war effort. The all-Japanese "442nd"—America's most decorated regiment—was unmatched in the proportion of casualties it suffered, and Americans of Japanese ancestry also served with distinction in the Military Intelligence Service.

Yet the internment went beyond the demands faced by all U.S. citizens during the war. The internment cost us three years and much more—not to further the defense of our country, but to cater to racial prejudices and political cowardice.

The internment amounted to the robbery of thousands of American citizens and residents—by their own government. Needlessly they were robbed of freedom, property, opportunity, and honor.

By lumping together all forms of wartime misery, many ignore the fact that the internment was a domestic act of theft and not an international expression of war. The internment never involved combat or conflict between wartime enemies. Today, too many people mention the attack on Pearl Harbor as if it somehow justified the internment. Such references neglect the fact that the internees were not Japanese nationals; but were native-born American citizens and law-abiding residents.

Of course this is not the first time our citizenship has been overlooked. In 1942, U.S. officials euphemistically labeled us "non-aliens."

Yet when I recall that period, I also thankfully remember that my parents succeeded in reminding me and my brother and sisters that we were Americans. Just before we were evacuated, my father gathered us in our living room and told us about rumors that all people of Japanese ancestry who were not born in America could be expatriated in exchange for U.S. prisoners of war. We children understood that our parents could be sent back to Japan. But even then, our father reminded us: Referring to San Jose, he said, "No matter what happens, this is your home."

That episode reminds me of more than the breach of our citizenship. Recalling my parents—the wartime loyalty they displayed and the trauma they endured—now reminds me that the internment was a shattering assault on a fundamental legal right. During the internment, our President, Congress, and the Supreme Court all used ethnic background as a standardized measure of loyalty. Our government thus abridged the fundamental right of each person to be judged as an individual.

The internment's dependence on an "imprison-by-background" policy is itself absolutely condemning. Even if we lacked the overwhelming evidence gathered by the Commission—evidence that there never was a "fifth-column" threat, the violation of rights still would leave the policy worthy of our condemnation.

Now there is widespread agreement that the internment was wrong. The remaining controversy about proposals for compensation centers on questions about whether it is wise now to seek reparations for a 40-year-old injustice.

One consistent hesitation about reparations is that they would set off on what lawyers call the "slippery slope" of precedent. "If we offer reparations for this," some ask, "will the American government be liable for all past government injustices?"

But the courts and the American government already have provided far more generous precedents for federal redress. In some cases, such as those affecting native American Indians who unjustly lost property, several hundred people collectively have received several million dollars.

The Commission recommendations and the World War II Civil Liberties Violation Redress Act limit the recipients to those who were interned, so that paying reparations in this case would provide no precedent for an endless, generation-hopping quest to redress all historical injustices.

A few have said that they want reparations determined in the courts and not in Congress, but then people have forgotten that the sudden internment seldom allowed for the derivation of tidy contracts or the careful collection of documents. If there had been time then, perhaps trials would be appropriate now.

Some people simply recoil at the figure of $1.5 billion, giving the estimated 60,000 survivors $20,000 each. But considering inflation and an annual interest rate of only 3 percent, economists working for the Commission estimated the total value of the material losses suffered by the interned would be $2.5 billion to $6.2 billion in today's dollars.

That figure does not include even an estimate of what is lost in years of forfeited freedom. Given the scope of these losses, the proposal for compensation of $1.5 billion is modest.

If you are skeptical about reparations, try to guess the amount of money that would prompt you into an agreement to sacrifice most of your property and to live in a prison camp for two or three years. And ask yourself how you would feel if this country incarcerated you and your family solely because of your ethnic background.

Would you seek redress?[35]

Righting an Old Wrong
Senator Alan Cranston (D-Calif.)

When the Commission on Wartime Relocation and Internment of Civilians recently reported, it addressed an issue in which I've been involved since the very beginning.

Shortly after Pearl Harbor, I was assigned to the Office of War Information. There I worked closely with Eleanor Roosevelt and Archibald MacLeish trying to dissuade President Roosevelt from forcefully evacuating Japanese-Americans from the West Coast and interning them in so-called relocation camps.

Unfortunately for 120,000 Japanese-Americans—and for the

good name of our nation—military authorities prevailed, and the orders for internment were issued.

More than two-thirds of the internees were American citizens. The rest were legal U.S. residents.

After the internment process began, I visited two of the camps, California's Tule Lake and Wyoming's Heart Mountain.

For four days in the cold snow-covered camp at Heart Mountain, I spent my time round-the-clock inside the barbed-wire camp, talking to internees and visiting with a number of my boyhood friends from Los Altos.

We ate meals together, talked over old times, walked around in the bitingly cold weather, played poker (in wanton violation of camp rules!) and danced together at a football rally.

My friends and former classmates justifiably felt themselves robbed of their citizenship. They were distressed at the racial prejudice behind their internment. They were anxious for their government to prove its own adherence to democracy and to the very ideals for which it was then at war.

President Roosevelt himself proclaimed, "In vindication of the very ideals for which we are fighting this war it is important for us to maintain a high standard of fair, considerate and equal treatment for the people of this minority as for all other minorities."

But this standard was not upheld.

The mere presence of Japanese blood in loyal American citizens was believed enough to warrant removal and exclusion for places they otherwise had a right to go.

The argument that they were removed for their own good, because of possible vigilante attacks was not persuasive. Most, if not all, Japanese-Americans would rather have faced the risk of being killed by individuals than deprived of their liberties by their own American government. And given the choice to remain interned or fight in the war, most enlisted and served.

One of my most poignant memories is of an intelligent and progressive—minded mother who was still managing—with much difficulty—to conceal from her four-year-old that they were prisoners in what most inmates considered a racial internment camp.

It was an ironic sight to see American Nisei soldiers, home on furlough and clad in uniform, wandering around inside a fenced-in camp. These Nisei soldiers were to return from the battlefields of Europe as the most distinguished and decorated combat unit of the war, and from the Pacific Theater as loyal soldiers and as officers in military intelligence. I have never forgotten these impressions.

I have always believed that our government's action in this case was a terrible affront to the ideals for which this nation stands.

In 1980, I was a co-sponsor of the legislation establishing the Relocation Commission. The report issued [in 1983] amounted to our government's official apology—41 years overdue—to the internees and their families.

The Commission report confirmed what a great many conscientious Americans have long believed: these Americans of Japanese descent were clearly mistreated, and their basic civil liberties violated.

The ACLU called the internment and related abuses of the time "the worst single wholesale violation of civil rights of American citizens in our history."

As one commentator on the period said, "Japanese-Americans were the immediate victims of the evacuation. But larger consequences are carried by the American people as a whole. Their legacy is the lasting one of precedent and constitutional sanctity for a policy of mass incarceration under military auspices. This is a result of the process by which the evacuation was made. That process betrayed all Americans."

The U.S. government carried out its policy without the benefit of reviewing individual cases or providing due process of law, and continued its policy virtually without regard for individuals who had demonstrated loyalty of the United States.

Not a single documented case of espionage, sabotage or fifth column activity was committed by Nisei or by resident Japanese aliens on the West Coast. Yet their lives were disrupted, fortunes were lost, and loyal citizens and legal residents incarcerated.

They were held collectively guilty, and collectively punished.

Moreover, the government's attitude toward these innocent people fostered suspicions that often led to violence against them and many were attacked when they attempted to return to their homes three years later.

This episode in American history should never have happened. It's the government's responsibility to set the record straight and to try, at least, to recognize and partially compensate for past injustices, although the tarnish of our Constitution can never be completely removed.[36]

DON'T PAY REPARATIONS TO INTERNED JAPANESE-AMERICANS

[In 1986, Congress will be debating redress bill HR 442, which calls for a formal apology by the U.S. government for the unjust incarceration of the approximately 120,000 persons of Japanese ancestry, and a payment of $20,000 for each survival incarcerated during World War II.]

The $20,000 Apology

I completely disagree with "The $20,000 apology." I also disagree with the Congressional Commission that recommend that $20,000 be paid to each of the survivors of the Americans of Japanese ancestry who were confined in relocation camps during World War II.

I have a number of friends who are Americans of Japanese ancestry and who also served in those camps. The important question, however, is how far back do you go in history to rectify wrongs or years is now a part of history. What about American Indians? The U.S. government mistreated most of them so badly and are still mistreating them. Are we going to try to rectify any of those grave wrongs?

What about the American blacks? Do you think that the white people in America realized that for all practical purposes all blacks in America are descendents of slaves and the vast majority of those are descendents of slaves into the 19th century? I can assure you the blacks are aware of the historical injustices that were committed against them.

I wish with all my heart that the relocation of the Americans of Japanese ancestry had not happened. But I also wish that Japan had not starved and slaughtered forty million to fifty million Chinese and several other million nationalities which the American Japanese had nothing to do with. I wish the Germans had not slaughtered six million Jews, twenty million Russians and several millions of other nationalities which the American Germans had nothing to do with.

My wish list could go on and on and on. But there can be no peace on this planet if we go back and try to rectify historical wrongs. I think that if Congress pays this money, the American taxpayers who will be footing this bill (many of who were not even alive in World War II) will resent it and it will have an adverse affect on Americans of Japanese ancestry.

It's important that we not repeat historical injustices. But to single out one group that has not received as harsh a treatment from the American government as some, we are really begging the whole subject of fair play to everyone.[37]

Reparation—Bad Precedent

I read with dismay the recommendation that more than $1 billion be paid by the U.S. government to those Japanese-Americans now living who have survived internment.

We can perhaps all agree after all these years that internment constituted overreacting. But was it legally unjustified in view of the Japanese sneak attack?

As an attorney, I believe that to pay "reparations" could set a bad precedent. What group will be next—the American Indian, displaced from his land after treaties were violated; the black who both before and after the Civil War has suffered repression; the German-American against whom recriminatory actions were taken during World War I and II? What makes the situation of the Japanese-American so special?

I suggest that the Japanese-Americans who feel aggrieved consider this: As a result of their internment, their parents or other relatives were safely shielded from service in the U.S. armed forces. None of them thus had to suffer injury, mutilation, or the ultimate sacrifice of death to defend this country against a war initiated by their forbears and or relatives in concert with Nazi Germany.

I hope that the Congress will view this issue in proper perspective and not seek temporary political advantage by passing legislation to implement the committee's recommendation.[38]

Survivor of Bataan March

I cannot believe that our government is going to pass a bill to pay $20,000 to Japanese-Americans who were put in internment camps during World War II.

My stepfather was a survivor of the Bataan death march and then was put into a POW camp in Japan.

He was forced to work in the coal mines from sunup to sundown. He was given three cups of tea and one cup of rice a day. He was in this camp from the time he was seventeen until he was 21.

When he was liberated from this camp he weighed 90 pounds. (He was 5 feet, 11 inches.) He was full of diseases. For all of this he was given his back pay of a little more than $3,000 for four years of misery.

If anyone deserves $20,000 it would be our fighting men who were in POW camps during the war, not some people who were here safe, certainly not being forced to work for nothing and being starved.[39]

JUSTICE DENIED: THE CASE FOR REPARATION

Japanese Americans Deserve Redress

I do not deserve a cent since I wasn't even born then. Whether my parents and other Japanese-Americans deserve redress, I don't know. I am writing to respond to the Monday-morning quarterbacks who wrote letters taking a firm position of no redress.

One person wrote that the Japanese-Americans don't deserve money since they were tucked away securely in the camps while American soldiers were dying on foreign soil. Just tell that to the interned parents of the Japanese-American soldier who was posthumously awarded the Congressional Medal of Honor while serving in the highly decorated 442nd, a Japanese-American unit that fought in Europe and has the highest casualty rate in the history of American armed forces.

Another writer told about the attack on Pearl Harbor and of atrocities committed by the Japanese on Americans during World War II. But what does that have to do with my parents and others like them? Does that justify me to say all German-Americans are bad because of the atrocities committed to 6 million Jews?

I'll agree with the Monday-morning quarterbacks that no redress is necessary if they will go to an internment camp with only what they can carry, not knowing what the future holds.[40]

Fighting For This Country
  I am the daughter of a Gold Star mother interned in Heart
Mountain, Wyoming. During the war, she sent off five of her
sons—my brothers. Out of the five, one was killed fighting for
this country. Another was wounded. There were many who served
their country this way. Need I say more?[41]

Reparation or Being Wrongly Imprisoned
  I can't understand the protests against paying American citizens reparation money for being wrongly imprisoned. Regardless
that they were of Japanese nationality, they were Americans
wrongly accused. They had less than a week to dispose of treas-
ured heirlooms, family belongings and homes.
  If you were surrounded by paranoid people, to whom would you
entrust your belongings? Your business and accountings? The
sale of your residence? Would you consider barbed wire a protection, or a prison? Internees carried few belongings into their
camps.
  Their treatment during World War II, by a nation such as ours
that holds itself up to be civilized, was unforgivable. Families
with German roots were not imprisoned or "interned."
  The issue here is treatment of American citizens and people
within the United States during World War II, not the march in
Bataan, not slavery, not racial prejudice.[42]

Will We Live to Receive Redress?
  I, now 82 years old and in poor health, am wondering if reparations will be received for the 1942-1945 internment of the
Japanese-Americans.
  Throughout the year, [1985] I have listened to fine words regarding the preservation and protection of the Constitution and
human rights. Now I ask myself if these words will bring even
a small fruition for the brutal violations of our constitutional
rights experienced during the internment.
  Many senior citizens lacked medical and mental [health] care
while in camp. This led to their early deaths. Those of us who
survived are sentenced to a shameful and humiliating life. Will
the government wait until we are all dead before they approve
our demand for redress?
  "Sleeping Sam" Hayakawa's [former senator from California]

intense desire for self-glorification and egomania limelight has been most unnerving, knowing the presence of prejudice against the Japanese-Americans. He has made such insulting remarks as, it make his skin crawl that we could seek redress—reparations for the incarceration.

I believe he said this in the hope that the populace would rally behind him. Failing, he claimed that those who returned from camp have made a success of their lives [and] that should be redress enough.

Unfortunately, he . . . does not go further to explain that over one-half of those who returned from camp are now dead, that the majority of us who are alive are preforming labor jobs, that only a small percentage are doing well.

Lately, "Sleeping Sam" said the the Japaneses-Americans are the most successful minority. He does not explain that most wealthy were born subsequent to 1945, making them far removed from the incarceration episode. To say we are well-educated, in fairly good jobs, businesses and professions is so irrelevant.

He went on to say that he is afraid of backlash. We don't need his advice or sympathy.

Last year (1983) at the Los Angeles Senate committee [hearing], Hayakawa spent his own time and money to negate our demands. He made a long, spirited oratory against redress. Those who heard him said that if he were in a speech contest, he would have won the national championship.

We oldsters wish to give "Sleeping Sam" some good advice. Man, you are pushing 80 years. All those years you have told us what you thought of us, what we should and should not do. Your fantasy as judge, god and dictator over us is over. No one accepts you as such.

You have had your glory as the no-nonsense president of San Francisco [State] University and [as] a U.S. senator. Enough of your egomaniacal hopes and desires! Yes, we have seen you with your tam-'o-shanter, always trying to get in front of the camera at the Republican meetings.

Don't climb on top of a stack of tofu—it just can't be done (a Japanese idiom).[43]

If No Reparation, Whose Rights Will Be Next To Go?
Bill Fukuba

Payment of reparations to interned Japanese-Americans is the proper amelioration response to the injustice of a government interning its own citizens for reasons of ethnic prejudice during World War II. This decision of the Congressional Commission on Wartime Relocation and Internment of Civilians was applauded by many.

It seems that [those who are opposing monetary compensation to the victims] have not been listening very carefully, [for] those who discount the Commission report, "Personal Justice Denied," by stating POW's suffered much harsher treatment in the hands of our enemies than the Japanese-Americans in internment camps. This is confusing the issue because the United States government was not responsible for the criminal behaivor of the Japanese and German leaders during World War II. Those responsible for the crimes against humanity were executed by hanging.

In case of the internment of Japanese-Americans our involvement is with the constitutional laws and the Bill of Rights and, rather than the degree of physical suffering, whether this episode in our history should have occurred at all.

The Commission's concern is the possibility of remedial legislation to correct a needless violation of constitutional rights and the advisability of additional measures to discourage future transgressions upon the Bill of Rights. Those who have been entrusted with protecting our individual freedom also bear the burden of seeing that our heritage of American democracy is passed on to posterity.

"We have learned nothing from history if the withdrawal of the First Amendment rights from German-Americans during World War I was followed 25 years later" . . . "with summary sanctions against an ethnic group on a scale unknown in our history . . . the internment of Japanese-Americans. "The quotation is from "Personal Justice Denied."

It would be highly irresponsible of our elected officials if they did not seek effective ways to ensure that such an invasion of personal liberty does not happen a third time. Those who argue against taking any corrective or remedial measures today because we cannot attend to all of the injustices of the past are in effect taking a position against progress and the hope for a better society.

Reparation is highly acceptable because it satisfies a two-fold purpose. It would be a meaningful restitution for losses suffered by those who were interned. More important, it would be a firm warning to those who in moments of passion might be tempted to usurp the freedom of whichever one of our minorities might be in disfavor at some particular time in the future.

In this nation of many different races, we are all members of one minority group or another. All of us are vulnerable, easy prey to the whims of the day were it not for the protective shield of our Constitution and our heritage of history.

Whenever a step is taken to add to the confidence that we and the generations to come will remain free, whenever safeguards to freedom have been secured and whenever the cause of liberty has been strengthened in any way, we all benefit.

[There] are claims that internment shielded Japanese-Americans from serving in armed services. Not true. Japanese-Americans were drafted out of internment camps in large numbers. The per capita number of Japanese-Americans serving in World War II was among the highest of any group, higher than the national average. The 100th Battalion and the 442nd Regimental Combat Team, composed entirely of Japanese-Americans, suffered the highest casualty rate of any group. Shielded from the U.S. military service? Japanese-Americans [suffered and received] more than our share of mutilations and the supreme sacrifice of death.

Another dissenter [against reparation], repeats the discredited argument that Japanese-Americans were interned for their own protection. Is it not twisting reason and logic to the point of absurdity to suggest that 110,000 law-abiding people should be locked up for protection from a handful of lawbreakers? Rumors and threats may have been prevalent, but there were only a few isolated cases of violence against Japanese-Americans. Oddly, the culprits were mostly non-whites.

The simple truth is that selfish economic interests on the West Coast succeeded in driving out the Japanese-Americans by using racial prejudice and war hysteria for their own self-serving purposes.

A word of explanation is due lest people get the wrong impression from many asserting that the internees received "adequate housing, wholesome food, medical attention, ample sanitation and recreational facilities." After the initial trauma of being uprooted from our homes we faced another jolt when we were headed into assembly centers.

At Portland, adequate housing meant 2,000 people packed into one large building with gunny sacks to be filled with straws for our mattresses. At Pinedale, ample sanitation meant no toilet facilities except smelly outhouses and community bathrooms with overhead pipes punched with holes to serve a showers. At Tanforan, one internee's first meal consisted of two slices of discolored cold cuts, overcooked Swiss chard and a slice of moldy bread. In all centers, medical facilities were primitive at best. Of course conditions improved when the WRA took over. Much of the improvements, however, came about through our own patient efforts.

Degrading and unpleasant as internment was, what set this event apart from other occurrences is that never before was such a wholesale disregard of constitutional rights promulgated as it was under Executive Order 9066. A dangerous precedent was established and still remains unrepudiated.

Finally, after [more than] 40 years, a congressional committee is recommending a sensible conclusion to this shameful chapter in American history. Failure to carry out this act of repudiation might leave the individual freedom of all citizens in a permanently precarious position.

Now is as opportune time as any to prove to ourselves and the rest of the world that such a gross disregard of civil liberties as took place in 1942 will not happen again in these United States.[44]

Address To The San Jose City Council
May 17, 1984
Councilman Jerry Estruth

If 120,000 American citizens were rounded up today and herded off to Detention Camps, the public outcry would be deafening. No court in the land would permit it and no governmental body or newspaper would support it.

Yet, scarcely 41 years ago, almost 120,000 American citizens were deprived of their Constitutional guarantees of due process and without fanfare were forced from their homes, farms and businesses. These citizens and their families were sent to camps where most of them were interned for the duration of World War II. Many of them were residents of our own valley and yet, our governmental bodies and local papers did nothing to help them.

Several weeks ago, [1983] I attended a dinner commemorating the 41st anniversary of the signing by President Roosevelt of Executive Order 9066 with hundreds of Japanese-Americans, I realized, perhaps for the first time, that I needed to understand a great deal more about what happened during those months in 1942 when many of these same people and their families were hustled off to distant and desolate places, deprived of their freedom, properties, Constitutional guarantees, and dignity.

I realized, too, I went all the way through San Jose's schools, graduated from Stanford, and got elected to the City Council without really having any consciousness of the grievous wrong which our country did to a defenseless population.

As a local elected government official, I was also interested in finding out what response our local governments and centers of influence made when the Constitutional guarantees of many of their constituents were violated right under their noses.

In evaluating the events of those days, it is important to examine the tenor of those times.

Our country had been attacked by Imperial Japan at Pearl Harbor and found itself at war with Japan, Germany, and Italy. We, who had been only watching the gathering clouds of conflict, suddenly found ourselves on an emergency wartime footing. Nobody knew where the next attack would fall or how long the war would last. There were reports of countries being enslaved, not only in Europe, but in Asia and the South Pacific as well. Civilians, from all walks of life were volunteering to serve their country in any way they could.

Additionally, the military mobilized for a total war effort and essential to this effort was the protection of the Pacific Coast from invasion. The man put in charge of the West Coast defense was General J. L. DeWitt, who received high marks in his day for his handling of the evacuation of the Japanese-Americans. As Henry L. Stimson, Secretary of War, said in his introduction to the Final Report, Japanese Evacuation from the West Coast, 1942: ". . . Great

141

credit is due General DeWitt and the Army for the humane yet efficient manner in which this difficult task was handled. It was unfortunate that the exigencies of the military situation were such as to require the same treatment for all persons of Japanese ancestry, regardless of their individual loyalty to the United States. But in emergencies, where the safety of the nation is involved, consideration of the rights of individuals must be subordinated to the common security. As General DeWitt points out, great credit is due our Japanese population for the manner in which they responded to and complied with the orders of exclusion."

In General DeWitt's Letter of Transmittal to the Final Report, he asserts without any sort of substantiation, that "thousands of American-born Japanese had been sent to Japan to receive their education and indoctrination," that "emperor worshipping ceremonies were commonly held and millions of dollars had flowed into the Japanese imperial war chest from the contributions freely made by Japanese here, "and that the continued presence of a large, unassimilated, tightly knit racial group, bound to an enemy nation by strong ties of race, culture, custom and religion next to a frontier vulnerable to attack, constituted a menace which had to be dealt with. Their loyalties were unknown and time was of the essence."

These self-serving and misguided statements were written by General DeWitt almost a year and a half after the evacuation in what was clearly an attempt to justify his actions. He says these beliefs caused his recommendation to the War Department which was made into Roosevelt's Executive Order. Consequently, our Japanese-American neighbors, [and absolutely no attempt was made to differentiate between non-resident aliens, resident aliens, or United States citizens of Japanese descent], were rounded up, herded off and disappeared from our midst. Where were our leaders and what did they do?

Looking at the historical record today, it seems that the real story is told, not by what is found, but by that which is not found. It seems that for our local elected bodies, it was a non-event.

The minutes of the Santa Clara Board of Supervisors and the San Jose City Council from December, 1941 to June, 1942, contain scant reference to the evacuation. The Supervisors noted and filed on February 24th, 1942, a Resolution from the County Supervisors

Association of California which urged immediate action be taken on the alien situation. After that brief mention, the only concern raised was on March 16th, 1942. The County was only interested in "assuming responsibilities, at Federal expense, for the relief of enemy aliens who have been required to move from the prohibited areas." Also on March 16th, 1942, great care was taken to order "that the County Welfare Department be authorized to assume responsibility for service to aliens of enemy nationalities. . . " Great care was to be exercised so that the County could be reimbursed by the Federal Government.

The San Jose City Council didn't even raise the issue of the evacuation. It didn't occur to our local government to ask whether or not such action was constitutional, legal, justified, or a violation of Civil Rights. Since the issue was not raised by any governmental official in our area, I can only assume that they did not perceive it to be a real issue.

In fact, the only reference I can find of any action taken by our local government regarding the evacuation was in June, 1943, when there was some talk about bringing the Japanese-Americans home from the camps before the end of the war. This time our elected officials took immediate action. On June 14th, 1943, our [Santa Clara] County Board of Supervisors unanimously voted to send a telegram to the Federal Government to protest the release of Japanese from the Relocation Centers.

Our City Council in San Jose did just a little better. On a split vote of 5 to 2, it voted to send the same telegram.

And what about some of the other leaders of San Jose? The San Jose Mercury Herald took a stand on Friday morning, March 27th, 1942. The Mercury Herald editorialized:

DO WE HURT AND CRUSH OUR ALIENS?
NOT WHEN GOVERNMENT IS JUSTICE

In this amazing editorial, the Mercury indicates that it is "extremely glad to see steps taken 'the American way' guarantee justice to this country." The paper is quick to point out however, "that great care will be taken to ensure that alien property is not damaged or stolen, or that the aliens themselves are not victimized by unscrupulous persons anxious to take advantage of their condition."

The editorial goes on to point out how "different this is from the policy of the axis powers" and asks us to consider the "plight

143

of the small farmers and businessmen of the Nazi occupied countries. In Poland, for example, these unfortunates were herded into starvation camps to become the prey to typhus, their possessions seized and given to the German Reich to be distributed as prizes to loyal party followers."

It exhorts us to broadcast a comparision of the two systems to the world. It points out that "one shows government at its best—a rule by justice. The other shows what we are fighting—government at its worst."

In the light of history, and I repeat that it has only been 41 years, these words seem self-serving and self-exculpatory at best, or deceitful, ignorant, and propagandistic at worst.

Some things are clear to me as a result of this brief investigation. It is clear that:

1) this country was involved in a war to ensure its survival;
2) the war effort enjoyed the massive support of the civilian population; and
3) in a very short period of time, the country geared up to support the military effort.

What is not clear, however, is how it was decided to suspend the Constitution of this country for people who were legally in this country, most of whom were United States citizens, and none of whom were charged with any crime or were found guilty of anything except having Japanese ancestors.

It is also clear that our institutions chose not only to ignore, but to endorse through their inaction, the actions that were taken and that either through fear, ignorance or prejudice, they chose to remain silent while their neighbors were sent to concentration camps by the United States government to house United States citizens.

CONCLUSION

This episode stands as a dark blotch on the history of the United States. It stains even darker when we stop to realize that it didn't happen hundreds of years ago or far, far away. It hurts even more when we realize that it happened here, in our own Valley, during many of our own lifetimes. And it was done, not by bad people, but people just like you and me.

The errors of our predecessors were not errors of commission, but rather errors of omission. Our leaders stood by while serious wrongs were committed and did nothing. We today are direct lineal descendants of those earlier Boards or Councils.

Do we not have a responsibility to right the wrongs of days gone by? I believe we do, and furthermore, we should right them in a way that will affirm human dignity to those who had it taken from them.

I believe that our San Jose City Council should take serveral steps:

1. We should declare that our Council erred when it failed to fight the evacuation. This recognition is important in a land where many history texts often don't even mention the event. We must put an end to the collective community of the chapter in our history.
2. We should appoint and fund a Council Commission directed to fully compile a record of what happened to our Japanese neighbors in the spring of 1942. This would include, but not be limited to, research on the conditions that led to the direct financial loss suffered by the Japanese-Americans, in San Jose, a compilation of a complete oral history of the evacuation in San Jose, and an investigation as to the effect on the citizenry in general.
3. This Commission should discuss and make recommendations regarding the type of redress desirable, possible forms of commemoration or memorialization, and what steps government should take to ensure that this never happens again.
4. Our City Council should throw its full weight and prestige behind any efforts needed to support redress an recognition resolutions in the United States Congress.
5. Our Council should learn from the past and resolve that this should never happen again, so that future Councils would learn from our efforts.
6. Our Council should support efforts to have the Supreme Court rehear the Hirabayashi, Korematsu, Endo, and the Min Yasui cases, which, according to many judicial sources are the worst Supreme Court decisions since Dred Scott.

In closing, it is important to remember that this did not happen long ago and far away. It happened here, in our city and was made to happen by those who lived here not too long ago. Let's resolve to never let it happen again.

(The above resolutions and recommendations proposed by then Councilman Jerry Estruth was approved on a 11 to 0, unanimous vote by the San Jose City Council, and Mayor McEnery was charged to appoint the new commission, which will be constituted as the San Jose Commission on the Internment of Local Japanese Americans.)

San Jose Councilman Seeks Internment Study
Jim Dickey

(Jerry Estruth, Councilman on the City of San Jose, California, on May 17, 1983 requested the Council to appoint a Commission to compile a record of what happened to local Japanese-Americans of San Jose in the spring of 1942. The Council approved the commission on a 11 to 0 vote.)

The Commission of ten to fifteen members will be appointed by Mayor Tom McEnery. Its work will include research on the conditions that led to the direct financial losses suffered by the Japanese-Americans, a compilation of a complete oral history of their evacuation from San Jose and an investigation of the effect on citizens in general.

The Commission also will discuss and make recommendations on the type of redress desirable, possible forms of commemoration, and what steps the government should take to ensure that such a thing never happen again in this country.

'Recognition is Important'

Estruth believes the City Council also should declare that the Council during the war years erred when it failed to fight the evacuation.

"This recognition is important in a land where many history texts don't even mention the event. We must put an end to the collective community denial of this chapter in our history," Estruth said.

He said he believes "we have a responsibility to right the wrong of days gone by" and "right them in a way that will affirm human dignity to those who had it taken from them."

Estruth worked with a committee representing a dozen Japanese-American organizations for six weeks before submitting the proposal to the Council. He went to the Japanese-American community. Its leaders did not come to him, and that's important, he said.

"It was important that an Anglo raised the issue. We did it to them, and we should rectify the mistake. We should restore the dignity we took from them," said the 40-year-old Estruth, who was not born until a year after the evacuation was ordered.

Richard K. Tanaka, the 50-year-old San Jose architect who headed the ad hoc committee that met with Estruth, agreed.

'Very Significant'

"We didn't solicit it, and that is very significant," Tanaka said, "It's like (Anglo-Americans) saying, 'We did wrong, and we're going to correct what we did wrong.' It's something more than we normally expect government to deal with. The government is people, and if the people are humanistic enough, they're going to deal with the issue. You could say it was that Council (in the 1940's) that did it, "therefore I don't have to deal with it."

Estruth said he grew up six blocks from San Jose's Japantown and went to school with Japanese-American kids but never knew about what happened to their families during the war.

"In America, we never talked about the Japanese-Americans. People just said, 'Well, they went away for the war,' " Estruth said.

Estruth majored in history at Stanford University, and even there his world history textbooks in 1962 never mentioned the internment of Americans in American concentration camps, he said."

Estruth said his experience in Germany as a 19-year-old student, when he visited the death camps, never left him, and he "came away with a real philosophical commitment to 'Never Again.' "

Estruth suggested that it may only have been the course of the war that prevented possible slaughter of the Japanese-Americans in the prison camps. It was said at the time that they were incarcerated for their own protection, but Japanese-American leaders have observed that the guns of the guards were pointed inward.

"The question has to be asked," Estruth said, "If the Japanese army had landed on the West Coast, what would we have done in the camps? Would the guards have turned the guns on the them? We rounded up American citizens, as Germany rounded up Jews who were German citizens."

Estruth said his office has received several hate phone calls from white San Joseans protesting the establishment of the Commission and wanting to know, "Why are you doing this for the Japanese?"

He said that many of the callers speak of loved ones killed in battles with Japanese military and see no difference between Japanese-Americans and the Japanese of World War II. Most of Americans (do not) see any different at the time, although Japanese-Americans were unquestionably loyal to America, Estruth points out.[45]

Chapter 11
THE NEW GENERATION,
A PRODUCT OF PAST EXPERIENCES

Social Behaviors

To western contemporaries living in the United States certain Japanese traits, phases and actions may seem strange, abnormal, non-individualistic and at times, appear to be weak in nature. Unless one fully understands these behaviors and traits, the observer may not be able to interpret the underlying essence of these actions.

A Japanese child growing up is given models to suggest property, and is taught to achieve to the highest levels of status, resulting, if accomplished, in great honors to one's family. The sense of independence or individualism, although important, is secondary to the image of the family. Therefore, certain predetermined acts of social behaviors are expected to be followed by all Japanese, and it is understood, that he or she naturally embrace these behavioral mechanisms.

One of the most important behavioral mechanism is the act of "haji," or shame. This concept of "What will others think of me?" "Have I achieved to my greatest potential?" "Am I the best in my class?" "What will the neighbors say?" All are behaviorial mechanisms which drive the Japanese youth and adults to succeed and ultimately to bring honor and greater image to the family and its namesake.

The shame orientation of "haji," peers judging you, in contrast

149

with a guilt of self-appraisal of an individual of one's personal action is an "effect" tool and mechanism designed to create social order and conformity. Due to the lack of spontaneous reactions by the Japanese on questions or issues being discussed, the Japanese-Americans often do not have the opportunity to share his or her thoughts, since the item under discussion may change to another new subject when he or she decides to volunteer a "correct or exact" answer to the previous question. Therefore, his or her input may never be shared with others.

This psychological reaction and hesitancy could be somewhat explained by the behavioral pattern of "enryo"; yet the individual in the Japanese society soon realizes that "keeping the mouth shut," especially, on unpleasant situations, or not volunteering or answering any question since it may possibly prove to be the wrong answer; all fortify the behavioral concept of "kuchi gotae sura na" (don't talk or answer back) in face of authority.

The family and the perception of others relative to its purported respect, image, honor and status are fundamental to the Japanese family unit. If one's son brought shame to the father and his family by becoming a "haitobo" (beggar) or a chorembo (bum), or even worse as committing a crime, this would destroy the family's social image. Therefore, the preservation of the family image though control of the patriarchial commandments is sternly emphasized, designed to make certain that shame will not be brought to one's family.

Sansei and Yonsei

The younger Sansei and the Yonsei of the 1980's are a product of protectionism of the hate and shame experienced by their past Nisei parents and Issei grandparents. The youth was shielded from the bitter experiences of "camp life," and it's moral degradation on their parents or grandparents for being incarcerated behind barbed wires during World War II (1942-1945). The parents feeling a sense of haji (shame) for being excluded from their home due to "military necessity"; imprisoned and guarded by armed guards; felt in essence being actual criminals. The parents of the Sanseis and Yonseis reasoned, "How can we raise my head high and be proud when we return, for we were criminals secured behind barbed wires?" "What will my plight be, when we return, after such an experience?"

"I can not share this with my children or grandchildren. I must blot this infamous portion of American history from our minds and go on. What good would it do to remind us of the tragedy of the evacuation and incarceration of we, American citizens?" Further, the returnees rationalized: "If we discuss or tell about our experiences, will it make our neighbors uncomfortable?" "This we must not do, for this is not a "Japanese" cultural trait, to make people uncomfortable! We must be pleasant and friendly at all times and hide our true feelings! Yes, we must forgive, but above all, forget. Yes, forget evacuation as if it never happened. It will be good for relations, it we serve the future generations of Japanese better, yes if we never bring it up, we will be certainly happier, and after all, we want to be liked, and never be hated or distrusted again. Our 442nd Nisei Regiment team during World War II has sacrificed their lives and limbs to prove to all that we are good Americans. Their sacrifices were far greater than ours, we will suffer only temporary mental anguish and sacrifice. This will go away in time, and last for only a short interim of time! Yes, let us forget, let us forget!"

These are collection of thoughts that were in most part the feelings of the majority of Japanese and Japanese-Americans returning from the relocation camps. They did not raise the question of this travesty that our government perpetrated, the unjust, and illegal incarceration, where due process of law was not exercised. "Military necessity?" "Why then, weren't the 'enemy aliens' of German and Italian decent not removed?" they asked.

The younger Sansei and Yonsei are generally achieving as well as their contemporaries. Living in a more affluent economic structure than their parents or grandparents, some Sansei and Yonsei are treating education at times as a social "in thing" to do, and are enthusiastic in pursuing their future occupations, professions or work. Yet some are confused on what direction they should take for their future endeavors which is one of the misgivings of many middle class white counterparts.

By the calculated efforts of the parents sheltering their tragedies and experiences of their "camp life," the Sansei and Yonsei are finding that there is a void in their lives. This void can be attributed directly to their parents not sharing their lasting psychological effects of their incarceration. Many of the camp residents never recovered from these tragic events, for many Issei

151

and Nisei residents are still carrying these experiences within themselves (not sharing with anyone) may answer the present voids or "non-experiences" in some of the personalities of today's Sansei and Yonsei.

In order to rectify and fill this void of "non-experience," the U.S. government must fully acknowledge and state that America has erred during this time. Only then, can this segment of society (who were wrongfully accused and never convicted of any crime, or tried under due process of the law; forced to sell property at fraction of the cost; all adding to the tramma of 1941), will be able to correct the psychological misgivings of the unjustified incarceration. Thus redress needs to be enacted immediately, so that future generations of Japanese-American citizens will not remain the only "void, non-experienced" citizens of the United States.

Sonsei/Yonsei, a Diverse Group
Peter F. Chen

"Sansei/Yonsei" is a diverse group of young people in American society which defies any generalization today. For nothing else, larger and larger number of children of Japanese-American parents are marrying non-Japanese-Americans, which immediately pose the question of which parent would dominate their cultural and ethnic identity. This identification varies and certain determination is based on the geographic locations where they are raised.

Taking "Sansei/Yonsei" of San Jose (California) as a whole, they seem to be in the period of a drastic transition (which incidentally has been experienced already in other areas). On the one hand, they are still pretty much categorized by their parental generation and also by the general society, (which tends to be more provincial) as typical American youths with very little cultural ties or influences similar to other Japanese youths in a number of other urban centers. [Yet] on the contrary, they are probably more influenced by their Japanese-American origin than they assume, both internally and externally.

Educationally, they are continuing to feel the pressure to succeed and are presently achieving and becoming successful, yet this strong direction has created untold tensions to some who are not geared toward the academics. Yes, they are more mindful of good citizenship, but rapidly becoming assimilated to the general life-style of the area.

I detect a growing frustration among the (Sanseis and the Yonseis) since they are not having the opportunity—to make great social and political contributions to the general society since these tasks are delegated to the hard-working middle class Niseis who have become involved with not only in the the greater community, but also have the definite ties with the Japanese-American community. We have a fine group of socially concerned Sanseis who are devoting much of their energies for the welfare of the Japanese-American community, but you seldom find them in the general arena (greater community). One exception, is in the business and educational sectors. Even there, "Sanseis/Niseis" tend to remain at middle management level.

They are in transition as they are struggling with their own self-understanding in dealing with the role in which they have been placed by the American society.

Random Thoughts on Sanseis and Yonseis

Ronald Y. Nakasone

It is difficult, if not impossible, to make general statements on the attitudes of Sanseis and Yonseis, the grandchildren and great-children of Japanese immigrants to the United States. Sanseis and Yonseis do not constitute a homogenous group. Chronological and geographical distribution has led to different experiences. Japanese have been immigrating to the U.S. since 1865 (Meiji-ganne); there is no single age group with which the Sansei and Yonsei can be identified. Senator Dan Inouye, for example, is a Yonsei. His outlook and attitudes are quite different from my Yonsei daughter, Heather, born in 1977. Children of Japanese immigrants who arrived after the Second World War, i. e., shin-Issei, are technically Nisei, but their attitudes and behavior patterns are more akin to mine, a Sansei's. Geographic distribution of the Japanese community had led to differnt responses to the American experience. The detention of the West Coast Japanese has left many of the detainees with a bitter legacy. The Japanese in Hawaii and those scattered in other parts of the U.S. are not as burdened with suspicion and fear of the American society and government.

153

In view of these problems, my remarks on Sanseis and Yonseis will be limited to those Japanese-Americans here in San Jose California, particularly with those associated with the San Jose Buddhist Temple. Sansei, [I] will refer to those are Japanese-Americans who were born shortly before, during and a few years after the World War II. They are in their mid-thirties to mid-forties and parents of the Yonsei children who attend our Sunday School. I do not believe that these parents represent the typical third generation Japanese. Association with a Buddhist institution already makes them unique.

There are far more Sanseis who are not associated with a Buddhist Temple. [Buddhist Churches of America (BCA) claims only 10,000 families out of an estimated Japanese-American population, according to the 1980 U. S. Census, of 791,2785.] Speaking in the broadest term, these temple attendee are well-educated, secure in their jobs, and relatively affluent. They epitomize the American success story. Many are from poor farming families, whose parents had little or no formal education. Through the encouragement of their parents and their own determination and education, the Sanseis have done well. Law-abiding, loyal and hard working, the Sanseis have attained positions of responsibility in both government and industry. They have all the trappings of the American middle class—a home in the suburbs, two cars, and respectability. Their children are the benefactors of the good life inheriting the attitudes and values of their parents.

The Sanseis can be characterized by a kind of romantic nostalgia for their ancestral past and culture. It is a past and culture which they know very little of and gained only through the memory of their grandparents and the traditions which they observe in the United States. The Temple is a reminder of their historical past and traditions: it is a repository of Japanese culture and the Buddhist faith.

The rememberance of things past and the appreciation and knowledge of one's cultural roots tie the Sansei to his/her heritage and ethnicity. The religious, cultural and martial arts clubs, the language school, and all the other groups associated with the Temple instill an identify, pride, and a haven from the mainstream American culture.

Parents readily admit that they want their children to mingle with their "own kind" and the Temple with its affililiated organizations provides the fellowship which they desire. The Temple, in short, is the focus of a Japanese-American ghetto, not physically perhaps, but spiritually and socially. (It should be noted that during the late 16th century, the Japanese, in the interest of profit, left for China and Southeast Asia in great numbers. The Chinese port of Canton had at one time as many as 40,000 Ryukyuans. In five generations, approximately 100 years, the Japanese population was completely assimilated into the local culture.)

Today, with 70 percent of the Japanese-American youth marrying non-Japanese, the Japanese-American community is quickly losing its racial identity. Sansei's inability to speak, read and write, [Japanese], I believe, is the cause of this rapid assimiliation. The traditions and rituals which the Japanese observe are preserved only in form (their original meaning has been lost.)

The Sanseis have been successful in American society because they are skilled in English. Mastery of this communication medium has allowed the Sanseis to be competitive in school and effective in the larger society. Their mastery of English has hastened their assimilation into the American mainstream and at the same time, distanced themselves from their historical and cultural past. Aware that their links to the past and their ethnicity are weakening, and wanting their children to have an appreciation for their rich heritage, the Sanseis made great efforts to involve themselves and their children with Temple and other Japanese related activities. The Sansei, as opposed to the Yonsei, has had some direct contact with their ancestral past through their grandparents. The Sanseis believe that there are much that they can be proud of and wish to enlighten their children of their ancestral roots.

There are many other Sanseis who do not attend the Temple. I know of a few, for example, who have no desire to identify [themselves] with other Japanese or care to know anything about their cultural heritage, and wish to assimulate as quickly as possible into the mainstream American society. These other groups, I am sure, possess different perceptions of themselves and the American experience.

Japanese-Americans' Changing Marriage Patterns

Japanese-American males who traditionally married Japanese-American females are changing their patterns. The traditional Japanese-American youths, Sanseis and Yonseis research states, will "alter" but not completely disappear as a "homogeneous, pure, ethnic group" (creating great concern to the Nisei parents) due to interracial marriages by the contemporary Japanese-Americans.

By pointing out variable signs along the way, Dr. Harry Kitano, who directed this study, speculates that by the year 2000, "only a small group of pure Japanese-Americans will exist as a group." He cites the following: "Half of the Japanese-Americans are thinking 'yellow is mellow,' and the other half are 'doing their own thing.' And perhaps, this is what America is all about."

Kitano, referring to figures from his book, *Japanese-Americans: the Evolution of a Subculture,* notes antimiscegenation laws have been enacted during the early history of America, and only nullified by the courts in recent years. Prior to the 1950's, Kitano states that Japanese in the Los Angeles area tended to marry within their own group. The Japanese outmarriages were 2 percent in 1924, since it was illegal during this period for Japanese to marry whites. By 1949, the rate was 11 percent, then up to 23 percent by 1959, and in 1977, it rose to 49 percent.

The statistics derived from the Los Angeles experience is not an isolated phenomenon. John Tinker's study indicated that outmarriage rate in Fresno (California) had jumped from below 20 percent through 1962 to 58 percent in 1969, and the Glen Omatsu's study of San Francisco's Japanese indicates that outmarriages rose from 58 percent in 1976 to 66 percent in 1977. In Hawaii, outmarriage rate was 47 percent in 1972. Therefore, in reviewing all the statistics from the various areas; indications are that outmarriages of Japanese are on the rise.

Although studies in Los Angeles, Fresno, San Francisco and Hawaii indicates that there seems to be a trend that the Japanese Americans are marrying out of the ethnic race, the 1970 U.S. Census do not confirm this trend. (The 1970 Census, indicates that 88 percent of Japanese marriages were to spouses of the same race.) The U.S. Census therefore contradicts the trend studies by Kitano, Tinker and Omatsu.

Kitano offers signs of basic changes in Japanese-American families. He points out the factors listed below as leading to the increase of Japanese outmarriages:

1. Opportunity for an "open contact", which is all time high today.
2. Group size, which if bigger lessens the prospect of outmarriage or, is smaller, furthers group change.
3. Sex ratio. Prewar, the inbalance favored the male. In 1971, there were more women, (319,000) females to (271,000) males.
4. Family structure, if strong will retain its Japaneseness. "Outmarriage is defined as marriages to anyone not of the same nationality group, including Asians. If "intermarriages" were counted, that is those to only non-Asians, then the rates will change to 49.9 percent for Japanese-Americans in 1979, in lieu of 60.6 which includes all "outmarriages" that is, Japanese-Americans marrying out of their own ethnic race. It is of interest that the Chinese-Americans and the Korean-Americans "outmarriages" in 1979 was only 41.2 percent and 27.6 percent respectively compared to 60.6 for Japanese-Americans.

The study further points out that in comparing the "intermarriages" between the Japanese-Americans to Chinese-Americans and Korean-Americans, again we find the Japanese-Americans are higher: 49.9 percent, compared to Chinese-Americans, 30.2 percent and Korean-Americans, 19.2 percent. Kitano acknowledges that his study do not take into consideration intermarried couples in the area who had been married out of Los Angeles County, since the basis of this report are statistics for the Los Angeles County's marriage records from the years of 1975, 1977, and 1979.

Kitano further states that even though his study do not include all intermarried couples, yet he believes that the results as reported is "90 to 99 percent accurate." The study also shows a consistent pattern that Asian women intermarried more often than men, and that American-born Asisan intermarried more often than immigrant counterparts.

The percentage of outmarriages of women were also higher than that of the men in all three years: 53 to 46 percent in 1975, 60 to 39 percent in 1977 and 52 to 47 percent in 1979.

Although Kitano's study is focused in the Los Angeles area, he thinks that if research was done in the other parts of the country, he will find that interracial marriages will be higher in areas where fewer Asians resides. Kitano said that the high rate of outmarriages among U.S. born Asians can partly be attributed to the fact that "the family can no longer control martial preferences," filial piety is eroding.

Therefore, the first generation preferences for marriage within the ethnic group is becoming weaker as subsequent generations become more acculturated, Kitano states. As noted earlier, Asian immigrants (Isseis) as well as their second generation offspring (Niseis) living in California were prohibited by law from marrying whites until 1948 and in general, faced much greater discrimination than today's third-generation Asian Americans. The third-generation (Sanseis) are generally highly educated, having usually a professional or a high paying job and having the same social opportunities open to them in the majority society, will as a whole depend less and less on their own ethnic community substructure.

On the basis of informal interviews with Asian American women, the study offers a possible reason why more Asians married non-Asians: a negative reaction to the tradition of male dominance adhered to by "old-fashioned males." Since Japanese-Americans at present, being the only Asian-American group in which the American-born outnumber immigrants, Kitano predicts that the outmarriages "probably will continue to rise. . .

Kitano states that at this time he considers that it would be premature to predict that Japanese-Americans will eventually disappear because of intermarriages. He says that new immigration from Japan may alter the reversal of this trend of Japanese-Americans intermarrying, or outmarrying, and notes that already many immigrant Japanese college students are choosing to live here.

Kitano concludes by commenting that he finds divergent patterns among American-born Nikkei (general term denoting all Japanese generations). "A sizable group still prefers other Japanese-Americans or Asians. You will also find quite a few saying they're just not used to associating with other Asians. Whatever direction the Sansei/Yonsei will take, will have a major impact on the traditional Japanese-Americans.

PLATE 9

Poston Relocation Camp, Arizona, 1942

Chapter 12
THE FUTURE HORIZONS

The Future

Evacuation, the removal and incarceration of a entire group, aside from being questioned to be unconstitutional and contrary to the spirit of justice, fair play and the American way, has changed irrevocably the social structure and pattern of a proud race. No more does the strict patriarch exist in a typical Japanese family; no more does the discipline of children being effectively controlled; no more does values and manners become an important observant; and no more does language and culture have significance or importance it richly deserves.

Issei

Due to the evacuation, the Issei lost his role as the head of the family or its breadwinner. The communal living and mass eating in large mess halls in the concentration camps tended to break down the vehicles for the teaching values and manners, and with the emphasis of "Americanization," language and culture no longer had any place in the total socialization process. Issei's leadership role in the community also diminished after his return, and due to his inability to speak English, hindered his assimilation process with the "white" counterparts. Therefore, the Issei who had lived a continuous life of suspicion, hate and jealousy, now has to live with this eroded dignity, and found the most devastating blow occurred when he lost his role as the patriarch of his family.

Christine W. Kiefer in *Changing Cultures, Changing Lives,* states that the Isseis "felt that they had been deficient in feeling and expressing loyalty to their host country" and are "not inclined to judge the relocation as unfair even when they recall the suffering and loss it brought them." Kiefer added, that many Isseis had elected to remain in this country after others had left in disgust. They were reluctant to admit that their gamble was a serious mistake, consequently rationalized in their minds that the evacuation was similar to a natural disaster, like typhoons and earthquakers of their homeland, very impersonal and therefore blameless, unavoidable, and somewhat accidental in nature, thus, psychologically they did not have to feel the guilt of self-betrayal.[46]

This form of rationalization can be explained by the phrase in Japanese: "shiga ta nai." I do not have any control over this matter—it is fate.

Nisei

The Niseis had experienced a different social psychological response to the evacuation experiences than the Isseis. Niseis experienced similar cultural and ancestral roots of their Issei parents, yet they thought of themselves to be Americans first, thus concluded that they were betrayed by their fellow Americans. They realized that their constitutional rights were taken away when they were placed behind barbed wires, and further concluded that the Japanese ancestry was the only reason for this injustice.

After World War II, the Nisei took over as the patriarch of his family, or its extended family (son or son-in-law of the Issei) due to the change of social behavior. The second generationn Japanese became more visible in public, began working to remove the past stigma of disloyalty, secrecy and distrust caused by the previous Issei's isolationist social behavior.

As noted earlier, many Niseis are believed to have lost faith in "white America," due to their traumatic experiences behind barbed wires. They reasoned that they are Americans, yet were betrayed by their white counterparts. Niseis, the "quiet Americans," turned these aggressions inward, although not blaming themselves as their Issei parents have done, made up their minds that they would change the self perceived public image of racial inferiority, by concentrating more feverishly to succeed economically.

By their hard work and sacrifices, the Nisei did succeed, thus was able to direct and educate his or her Sansei offspring and to announce to America: "We are as good or better than all of our fellow young Americans." Although the Nisei parents directed the Sansei offspring in this postive direction, the Sansei started to question the non-sharing of their parents' experiences of their plight of incarceration. The Sansei/Yonsei will soon create a movement to highlight and focus this tragedy, so that all Americans would acknowledge this painful experience. The Isseis and Niseis' desire to hide or not talk about these suppressed experiences is an act of practicing "social amnesia." Dr. Tetsuden Kashima comments that this is a "group phenomenon in which attempts to suppress feelings and memories of particular moments or extended time periods . . . a conscious effort . . . to cover up less than pleasant memories."[47]

Sansei and Yonsei

The Sansei, the offspring of the Niseis are portrayed as the "most successful model minority in the United States." They are successful achievers, free from some of the social pathology of their parents. Most Sanseis did not experience the incarceration behind barbed wires, yet are only today, understanding these experiences, since their parents are becoming more open and finally sharing their experiences of incarceration.

The majority of the population in relocation camps, were Isseis, with older Nisei offspring or Nisei with young Sansei children, and very few if any, Sansei parents resided in relocation camps. The Sansei parents today have Yonsei offspring. Even though most Sansei and Yonsei did not experience the "camp life," they are a product of their parents' and grandparents' psychological and physical experiences. The Sansei/Yonsei were directed by their parents to become well-educated in order to guarantee their success, and were purposely protected and devoided of any experiences of the incarceration of their parents.

The parents refused to acknowlege the psychological and physical losses existed by simply stating: "Let's forget about it, it doesn't matter anyhow." It is now reported, that these hidden

PLATE 10

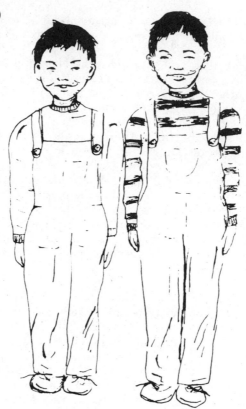

Two small boys sat on the log; coals glowed in the tub before them.
"Are we Americans," asked one.
"No, we are not Americans," his friend answered.
"But we were born here, if we are not Americans, what are we?"
"We are human beings."
"Who are the Americans?"
"White people are Americans."[51]
If injustice was perpetrated, if incarceration was directed without due process and with the usurping of one's constitutional rights, then proper redress and governmental apology must be the natural course and the proper agenda.

thoughts are now having certain impact on the Sansei/Yonsei group. The void now being surfaced by the younger generation may explain some of the behavioral patterns of today's youth. Some of these offspring, although successful academically, socially yet psychologically felt this void, and could not till recently explain certain behavioral patterns which they could not understand, yet through research and questioning their parents and grandparents are experiencing and learning for the most part these void experiences from their parents.

The Sansei/Yonsei are finally being sensitized with the experiences of the evacuation, where their parents and grandparents were made prisoners, incarcerated for more than two and a half years, convicted of no crime or tried in a duly constituted court. This unjust removal of a total ethnic group from society has caused undue financial as well as psychological damage, since the Issei and Nisei parents even today, feel a sense of shame (haji), yet collectively after the World War II, and their subsequent return to California, made an unwritten pact to "forget it, don't make waves we must bear this," (gambaru), for they felt that the important issue is the welfare of future generations of Japanese-Americans to come. With respect to Japanese culture, these behavioral patterns were intended to reinforce family honor and image. These behaviors, somewhat explain partially the rational of keeping these somewhat traumatic experiences of the parents away from the young generations.

For Japanese-Americans, camp is a point of reference. As one Sansei/Yonsei states:

> I can go anywhere in the United States today and . . . talk to a Nisei or Japanese-American family and after the initial social amenities are taken care of . . . discussions . . . without a doubt . . . will get to the topic of camp. . . . People will ask, "Were your parents in camp?" And if you tell them what camp your parents were in, and if they were not themselves in that camp, then they would ask if you know so-and-so who was in that camp.[48]

Due to its painful memories, interned Japanese-Americans avoided discussing their experiences of camp and camp life, yet, when they occurred at all, for a long time, only the trivial or humorous moments were shared. The Sansei sometimes found this troubling:

> When I first learned of the internment as a youth. I found that it was a difficult matter to discuss with my parents. My perception of them was that they did not speak honestly about the camp experience. Positive aspects were always seemed to be something that was left out. My feeling was that there was much more to the experience than they wanted to reveal. Their words said one thing, while their hearts were holding something else deep inside.[49]

What were the consequences or adverses effects on the Sansei and the Yonsei? This void and their partially missing sense of being, experienced by the Sansei and Yonsei offspring, may be possibly traced to the "covering-up" and the non-sharing of their parents' experiences.

This missing link, the denial of the parents not sharing their so-called "shameful demeaning experiences", (non-experiences) made many Sansei/Yonsei wonder what was lacking in their lives, and because of this, become somewhat unsure of themselves, resulting in carrying forth and intensifying the "enryo" social behavior, which is contrary to the so-called socially accepted middle class American behavior.

Harry H. L. Kitano in his definitive study: *Japanese-Americans: The Evolution of a Sub-structure*, states:

> "Enryo" helps explain much of this Japanese-American behavior. As with other norms, it has both a positive and negative effect on Japanese articulation. For example, take observations of Japanese in situations as diverse as their hesitancy to speak out at meeting; their refusal to second helping, their acceptance of a less desired object where given a free choice, their lack of verbal participation expecially in an integrated group, their refusal to ask questions; and their hesitancy in asking for a raise in salary—these may be based on "enryo." The inscrutable face, the noncommital answer, the behaviorial reserve can often be traced to this norm so that the stereotype of the shy, reserved Japanese in ambiguous situations is often an accurate one.[50]

Growing up with the social behavior of "enyro" and the "haji" shame syndrome, many Sansei/Yonsei offspring have not fully assimilated in the total American social fabric due to one's parents environmental and psychological experiences. Only today, the Japanese youth is understanding that he or she needs to and must carry on the burden of their parents or grandparents's experiences of incarceration, for only through the completion of this cycle, could they fulfill and this "void of non-experience." The combination of the void of "non-experience" and the cultural "enyro" behavior and the "haji" syndrome caused by the incarceration, all are contributing to the "lack of confidence," non assertive behavioral patterns displayed today by many Sansei and Yonsei siblings. How tragic and how far-reaching will be psychological effects affecting future generations of Japanese-Americans, only time will tell.

The Japanese-Americans challenge is still before us. Whether all Americans will acknowledge and understand the inequities and the injustices caused to a select minority in America, time will tell.

Whether it could happen to Japanese-Americans again or to a newly selected minority, history will report.

A Day of Remembrance

Each year as part of the Day of Remembrance commemoration (February 19, 1942), responsive members of the communities throughout the United States present a program on the reflections of the incarceration of 120,000 Japanese and Japanese-Americans in 10 concentration camps in the United States.

At the 1985 Day of Remembrance held in San Francisco, California, Chief Justice Rose Elizabeth Bird of the California Supreme Court offered a poem she had personally written for this occasion. This poem is dedicated and the current danger of scapegoating in this country and the need for people to protect the rights of minorities and the poor.

A Day of Remembrance—that is why we are here.
Remember when justice was once ruled by fear?

Remember when freedom was clearly your right
Provided you proved that your skin was pure white?
Imagine a horse stall with no light or heat,

No home, no possessions, no shoes on your feet.
Imagine the cold Utah desert at night,
No charges, no hearings, just government's might.
In General DeWitt's world, "a Jap was a Jap,"
So thousands were sent to 109 dots on the map.
Like Tule Lake, Manzanar, Topaz, Jerome,
Where freedom was forfeit and prison their home.

What happens to hope when your country betrays you?
What happens to dreams, is this how it repays you?
Within lies the strength to stand up to despair,
In our sense of self-worth and belief in what's fair.

The difference between an ideal and a right,
Depends upon someone to fight the good fight.
Depends upon someone to strive 'til they win,
So what happened before will not happen again.

It took 40 years to secure reparations
For Fred Korematsu and two generations,
But striving together, the young and the old
Achieved something more than a tale finally told.

Together, they went to the courts of this land,
To call on our conscience to come to the stand,
To peacefully gain an admission of error,
And wrest dignity from the camps' reign of terror.

A Day of Remembrance that burns like an ember.
Can it happen again. Yes—unless we remember.[51]

FOOTNOTES

1. Howard B. Melendy, "California Japanese, 1890-1941," (1984).

2. Jitsuichi Masuoka, "Changing Moral Bases of the Japanese Family in Hawaii," *Sociology and Social Research*, v. 21, no, 2, (Nov/Dec 1936), p. 162.

3. Ibid., p. 164.

4. M. Togo, "The Nippon Shokuminron," pp. 296271; also Okawahira, "The Nippon Iminron," pp. 3840.

5. "The Japanese-American Year Book," The First Appendix, (1901), pp. 3-4.

6. "A History of Japanese in Hawaii," Ed. by Publication Committee, United Japanese Society of Hawaii, Dr. James H. Okahata, Chm., Honolulu: The Toyo Shoin, (1938), pp. 214-15.

7. Forrest E. LaViolette, *Americans of Japanese Ancestry, A Study of Assimilation in the American Community* (Toronto: The Canadian Institute of International Affairs, 1945), p. 61.

8. *Honolulu Star Bulletin* (Sept. 21, 1931), 6:1.

9. Curtis B. Munson, "Report on Hawaiian Islands," in Pearl Harbor Attack, Hearings before the Joint Committee on the Investigation of the Pearl Harbor Attack, United States Congress, 79th Congress, 1st session, Part 6, pp. 26926.

10. Curtis B. Munson, "Pearl Harbor and Confinement," *Hawaii: End of the Rainbow* (Tokyo: Charles E. Tuttle, 1964), pp. 297-313.

11. United Japanese Society of Hawaii, p. 271.

12. Ibid.

13. Memo, Hoover to Attorney General (Feb. 2, 1942), (CWRIC 5794, 5796).

14. Grizzly Bear, (Jan 1942), reprinted in Morton Grodzins, *Americans Betrayed* (Chicago: University of Chicago Press, 1949), p. 48.

15. Letter, Leland M. Ford to Stimson, Jan 16, 1942, NARS. RG 107 (CWRIC 4376) ; Grodzins, *Americans Betrayed*, pp. 64-65.

16. Jacobus TenBrock, Edward N, Barnhart and Floyd Matson, *Prejudice, War and the Constitution* (Berkeley: University of California Press, 1954), pg. 75

17. General John L. Dewitt, "Final Report: Japanese Evacuation form the West Coast" (1942), pg. 34.

18. Report of the Commission on Wartime Relocation and Internment of Civilians, "Personal Justice Denied," Washington D.C.: (Dec. 1982). pg. 80.

19. Congressional Record (March 19, 1942), pg. 2726.

20. Henry Steele Commager, "Who Is Loyal to America," *Harper's Magazine* (Sept. 1947).

21. Personal Justice Denied, Report of the Commission on Wartime Relocation and Internment of Civilians, Washington D.C. (December 1982), p. 138.

22. U. S. Department of Interior, WRA, The Evacuated People: A Quantative Description, (1946), p.8.

23. Report of the WRA, p. 8.

24. Carey McWilliams, *Prejudice: Japanese Americans: Symbol of Racial Intolerance* (Boston: Little, Brown, (1945), p. 257.

25. "Internees in WW II Can Sue," *San Jose Mercury News* (January 22, 1986), p. 1.

26. Frank J. Taylor, "The People Nobody Wants," *The Saturday Evening Post* (May 9, 1943), p. 66.

27. H. Bruce Miller, "The Bigotry Bug Is Catching Again," *Jose Mercury News* (March 3, 1984), Section B.

28. Letter, Brad Wong to *Epitaph*, Homestead High School, Cupertino, California (Oct. 23, 1983).

29. "Pierman Convicted of Manslaughter," Report by East West, *Pacific Citizen* (Oct. 12, 1984), p. 1.

30. Jon Takasugi, Protestors, Supporters demand justice in race-related "murder" of Vincent Chin, *Pacific Citizen* (July 22, 1983), p. 1,8.

31. Poster at Six Flags Auto World, Flint, Michigan, reproduced from *Pacific Citizen* (Sept. 28, 1984), p. 2.

32. Poster, "Japan View Down the Gun Barrel," reprinted from the Chicago Tribune, *San Jose Mercury News* (June 17, 1985), p. 7B.

33. *Spartan Daily*, San Jose State University, San Jose (December 7, 1984).

34. Lowry Objects to Iococca's 'Nationalism', *Hobubei Mainichi* (April 13, 1985), p.1.

35. Norman Y. Mineta, "An American Tragedy and Reparations," *San Mercury News* (June 26,1983), Section C, p. 1C.

36. Senator Alan Cranston, "Righting an Old Wrong," *Hokubei Mainichi* (June 18, 1983), p. 1.

37. "Don't Pay Reparations to Interned Japanese Americans," The Letters Page/View of Mercury News Readers *San Jose Mercury News* (June 25, 1983), p. 7B.

38. Ibid.

39. Ibid.

40. "Justice Denied: The Case for Reparations," *San Jose Mercury News* (July 1, 1983), p. 11B.

41. Ibid.

42. Ibid.

43. Tom M. Nakaji, "Will We Live to Receive Redress?", *Hokubei Mainichi* (San Francisco: March 29, 1985), p. 1.

44. Bill Fukuba, "If No Repatations, Whose Rights Will be Next to Go?" *San Jose Mercury News* (July 1, 1983), p. 1.

45. Jim Dickey, "S. J. Councilman Seeks to Internment Study," *San Jose Mercury News* (May 27, 1983), p. 2B.

46. Christie W. Kiefer, *Changing Cultures, Changing Lives* (San Francisco: Jossey-Bass Publishers, 1974), p. 65.

47. Report of the Commission on Wartime Relocation and Internment of Civilians, Testimony, Tetsuden Kashima, Seattle (Sept. 11, 1981), p. 102.

48. Ibid., Testimony, Warren Tadashi Furutani, Los Angeles (Aug. 5, 1981), p. 167.

49. Ibid., Testimony, Michael Yoshii, San Francisco, (Aug. 5, 1981), p. 246.

50. Harry H. L. Kitano, *Japanese Americans: The Evolution of a Sub-culture* (Englewood Cliffs, New Jersey: Prentice-Hall, Inc. 1969), p. 104.

51. Chief Justice, Rose Elizabeth Bird, Supreme Court of the State of California, San Francisco (Feb. 23, 1985). Publisher Anderson, Ritchie & Simon.

52. Estelle Ishigo, *Lone Heart Mountain* (Los Angeles: 19723), p. 104.

INDEX

174